The Daily Telegraph

80 YEARS OF
CRYPTIC
CROSSWORDS

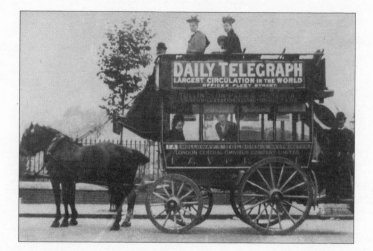

The Daily Telegraph

80 YEARS OF CRYPTIC CROSSWORDS

Val Gilbert

MACMILLAN

First published 2004 by Macmillan
an imprint of Pan Macmillan Ltd
Pan Macmillan, 20 New Wharf Road, London N1 9RR
Basingstoke and Oxford
Associated companies throughout the world
www.panmacmillan.com

ISBN 1 4050 4923 5

3 5 7 9 8 6 4 2

A CIP catalogue record for this book is available from
the British Library.

Printed and bound in Great Britain by
Mackays of Chatham plc, Chatham, Kent

Contents

The front-page headlines from 1913

Introduction

The Daily Telegraph crossword first appeared on 30 July 1925. The initial plan was for these new-fangled puzzles to be published for just six weeks in deference to a passing American craze. The rest, as they say, is history . . . In the intervening 80 years scarcely a weekday has passed without a *Daily Telegraph* crossword, and in that time it has matured from the simple crossword of 1925 to the current cryptic teaser that daily entertains and challenges a large chunk of the paper's readership.

In this book we have gathered together 80 crosswords – one from each year of *The Daily Telegraph* crossword's existence. Each ten years has its own preface, which attempts to blend in some of the events of that decade with the crossword's development. In 1975 *The Daily Telegraph* produced a crossword book to celebrate its 50th anniversary, and I am much indebted to the late May Abbott for the research she did for that book; the prefaces to the first four decades of this book are probably more her writing than mine.

Currently, *The Daily Telegraph* has a team of six crossword compilers – one for each day of the paper's

1

week – with four more individuals as occasional setters and emergency stop-gaps.

Peter Chamberlain compiles the Saturday puzzle. He became interested in crosswords as a boy, when he spent some time in hospital. Later, as a chartered accountant, he spent all his spare time compiling crosswords, becoming a professional 27 years ago. He has been on *The Daily Telegraph*'s team for 18 years, initially taking the Wednesday spot and moving to the prized Saturday position on the retirement of Alan Cash.

Ruth Crisp, who sets the Friday puzzle, probably the hardest of the week, is about to retire. Now in her mid-80s, she feels the time has come to hang up her compiling pen. She began creating crosswords professionally in 1955, after being forced to leave the Civil Service when she married. At one time she was working 16 hours a day, seven days a week, compiling puzzles to pay for her penthouse flat overlooking the sea at Westcliff in Essex. On Friday, 27 September 2002, we printed her 1,000th puzzle for the paper; the previous day that same crossword had tested the wits of the finalists in the first Bert Danher Memorial Crossword Competition.

Bert Danher, who had died earlier that year, had been responsible for the Thursday crossword for nigh on 25 years. A Liverpudlian and former music teacher, as befits a cousin of Paul McCartney, he played the French horn in amateur orchestras for fun. His crossword speciality was anagrams, which he composed with the help of Scrabble blocks. His Thursday slot has been taken over by his fellow Liverpudlian and friend Jeremy Mutch, who takes time off from his day job as an interpreter and translator to create crosswords.

Ann Tait supplies the Wednesday puzzle. A classicist, she taught Latin at a girls' grammar school in Gloucester before retiring to concentrate on her crosswording skills. She belongs to no particular school of crossword thought – to solve her puzzles you need a good grasp of language and reasonably good general knowledge. Ann Tait began her *Telegraph* crossword life as a Monday compiler, taking over from senior compiler Douglas St P. Barnard (more than 40 years of *Telegraph* crosswords) during a long illness.

The Tuesday crossword is compiled by Anne Campbell-Dixon, whose connection to the *Telegraph* goes back more than half a century – her father was the paper's film critic. She herself was one of the paper's television critics in the 1970s and then moved on to write travel and heritage features. She lives in the lowlands of Scotland and is a regular contributor to the *Telegraph*'s travel pages, as well as the back page on Tuesdays.

Roger Squires – actor and member of the Magic Circle – completes the *Telegraph*'s regular team by supplying the Monday puzzle. He lives in Shropshire and merits an entry in the *Guinness Book of Records* as the most prolific crossword compiler. He saw his one millionth crossword clue published in 1989 – happily, in *The Daily Telegraph*.

Four other compilers are called on from time to time: Dr Jeffrey Aronson, Oxford resident and member of the research team at that city's Department of Clinical Pharmacology at the Radcliffe Infirmary; Don Manley, also an Oxford resident and a professional crossword compiler, as is Mike Laws, London denizen and previously editor of *The Times* crossword. Raymond Terrell – currently a resident in Paris – makes up the quartet.

The geographic spread of the *Telegraph*'s compilers – Scotland, Liverpool, Oxford, London, Gloucestershire, Northamptonshire, Shropshire, Essex and the Continent – serendipitously almost mirrors the spread of the *Telegraph*'s readership (although, unlike the readership, we have no compilers representing Wales and Northern Ireland), with an emphasis on the south and east.

Most crossword compilers will tell you that their life is a lonely one. There is no compilers' association and they hardly ever meet. However, they probably have a more intimate relationship with newspaper readers than most other contributors. Many cruciverbalists (crossword fans) liken solving a cryptic crossword to a one-to-one gladiatorial contest – the solver versus the compiler – and develop an intense personal relationship with their daily puzzle, inventing a mental image of the compiler that may or may not accord with reality.

Many compilers originate as avid crossword solvers and most of *The Daily Telegraph*'s setters have a favourite cryptic clue. Peter Chamberlain favours one he first saw 20 years ago:

> **Clue:** 'You may have seen a cakewalk but have
>   you seen plenty of this?' (9)
> **Solution:** *Abundance*

Ann Tait likes:

> **Clue:** 'Lots of lucre but little luck' (5,7)
> **Solution:** *Small fortune*

Myself, I have always had a soft spot for Douglas St P. Barnard's (Monday compiler in the 1980s and 1990s):

> **Clue:** '   !' (4,3,3,1,4)

which, of course, has the answer *Have not got a clue*. Words that should not spring readily to your lips when tackling the 80 crosswords in this very special crossword book. Happy solving!

1925–34

The issue of *The Daily Telegraph* in which that first crossword puzzle appeared contained 18 pages and cost 2d (just under 1p). The main news concerned 'desperate last-minute efforts' made by the prime minister, Stanley Baldwin, to avert a stoppage in the coal industry. The miners were threatening to strike for a national minimum wage – this strike was the forerunner of the General Strike that was to grip the nation the following year. The weather on 30 July 1925 was also striking an appropriate note of gloom. *Hotspur* reported from Goodwood that the place was 'shrouded by rain and mist, lashed with all the furies driven in from the Channel – horrible, soaking and thoroughly inglorious'. In foreign parts Hindenburg had been elected president of Germany and the Prince of Wales, escaping from the domestic gloom, had set sail from Cape Town for South America. The diversion the paper provided for its stay-at-home readers was the day's instalment of its serial, *Christina Albert's Father*, by H. G. Wells. Enter the crossword . . .

The compiler of that first *Telegraph* crossword was

Leonard S. Dawe, senior science master at St Paul's and later headmaster of the Strand School at Tulse Hill, London – a portrait of him is housed at the *Telegraph*'s head office at Canary Wharf. The paper's acrostic expert said that he 'wouldn't touch crosswords with a bargepole'; just how Dawe came to be approached is lost in the mists of time. However it occurred, he accepted the challenge of creating something entirely new, for an untested readership in an untried market. The shape of the grid followed its American template, being vaguely suggestive of a piece of Axminster carpet. The puzzle, in fact, comprised nine small self-contained crosswords enclosed in a 15-letter square (not that dissimilar to American crossword patterns of the present day). The general knowledge content of the clues and solutions gave it the added interest of a popular quiz programme. Two-letter words, soon to be banished, were used liberally at first, and at this stage brand names were also acceptable. The puzzle was an immediate success.

In their first years the puzzles changed markedly, though not completely. Some of the cryptic clues gave a foretaste of the good things to come:

Clue: When they have them in the Reichstag the motion is defeated
Solution: *Neins*

On the other hand, some of the clues were so generalized that quite a range of answers could be equally applicable:

Clue: Wimbledon this looks beautiful
Solution: *Sod*

There were, too, the beginnings of that science of dissecting, analysing and reassembling words that was eventually to become so complex – although not always, at first, with very successful results:

Clue: Put its tail on its head and look for it in
    Richmond Park
Solution: *Stag*

During those early years just two compilers – Melville Jones, a classics master also at St Paul's, joined Dawe almost immediately – were responsible for all *The Daily Telegraph* puzzles. They got into the swing of it quite quickly, but hesitated to take their solvers along with them at the same pace – as is still true to the present day. For a long time the clues continued to be a mixture of cryptic and simple styles, usually with the cryptic clues dominating the *Across* section, and synonyms more apparent in the *Down* clues. Nor in this decade did the clues show how many letters the solution comprised (the solver had to count the squares).

To begin with, when many patterns followed the American style, too many white squares were massed together in some of the patterns. The frustration of trying to find words to fit, obviously drove compilers to despair. Obviously, because on occasions they used words that were not words at all. One can imagine the reaction of today's solvers to the clue 'This has its tail dislocated' on discovering the next day that *sthi* was indeed the correct solution, or finding that *ilfe* was the solution to the clue 'A muddled life'.

During this time, the compiler would state clearly that his solution was an 'Anagram', or 'Hidden', instead of disguising this fact as part of a cryptic clue. Sometimes the briefest of hidden words was buried in a long and irrelevant sentence, such as 'The appalling disasters caused by the floods loosened British purse-strings'. The solution – *heap* – is hidden in the first two words. And another example is even more unacceptable by present-day standards: ' "One shilling' was priced on each article (Hidden)' to which the solution was *Char* – the clue contained no hint as to why the answer should not be *ones*, *hill*, *ling*, *wasp*, *rice*, *iced*, *done*, *ache* or *hart*!

In March 1928, the first Saturday Prize Crossword appeared – they have continued ever since. In those early days the three weekly winners were offered their choice of books up to a value of two pounds. They selected the titles, and the books were duly sent to them.

Inevitably, this innovation gave rise to a new interest. People combed the lists of winners for recognizable names, while diarists turned their researches to the kind of book chosen as prizes by crossword competitors.

'They are obviously highly intelligent people,' commented Peterborough (the illustrious and long-lived father of the current 'Londonspy') in *The Daily Telegraph* of 11 November 1930. 'Lord Birkenhead's *Turning-*

points in History and John Langdon-Davies's *Man and His Universe* are typical selections; and in fiction Vicki Baum's *Grand Hotel* and Rose Macaulay's *Staying with Relations* seem to set the standard. One of the winners last week elected for Wickham Steed's book on Stanley Baldwin.'

Other diarists were interested in the kind of people who tackled the puzzles regularly, winners or not. Stanley Baldwin himself figured prominently among them as did Sir Austen Chamberlain and Lord Russell of Killowen, as well as eminent clerics and rural deans. The Prince of Wales, on the other hand, confessed that he 'was not very good at solving crosswords' – although both his and the Duke of York's private secretaries figured in the winners' lists.

In January 1930, *The Times* finally succumbed and published its first crossword puzzle. Meanwhile *The Daily Telegraph* compilers, with their five-year lead, were now exploiting to the full the double meaning and the illusory pun. Such joys as

Clue: A maker of conveyances
Solution: *Notary*

Clue: This may mean a flat rate for the motorist
Solution: *Puncture*

About this time the anatomy of words was coming under scrutiny and complicated surgical operations were starting:

Clue: As the motorist knows, starting without
    irritation is this
Solution: *Art* (removing the *sting* from *st-art-ing*,
    thus leaving *art*)

Clue: Many a one has had his prospects this
    through being last in bed
Solution: *Blasted* (i.e. putting *last* inside *bed*
    making *b-last-ed*).

Already in 1931, the techniques were being elabo-
rated. Words were decapitated, syllables turned head to
tail and more play was being made with abbreviations
and anagrams of the constituent parts of solutions. An
early example of this is:

Clue: You need two notes and a letter in your
    purse to be able to buy this
Solution: *Purchase*

Compilers were beginning to play with words read
backwards, upwards and the same in both directions.
They started using clues which 'soundly' echoed the
solutions with words of an unrelated meaning. But clues
were still a mixed bag with the pedestrian 'Anagram
of "blue man"' (Solution: *Albumen*), nestling beside the
aforementioned delights.

In the pioneering days of compiling cryptic crosswords it was much easier, of course, to be original. The
compiler was ploughing his furrow in virgin soil. No
doubt he was widely applauded for his ingenuity when,
for the first time, he used 'bloomer' for a flowering plant

or 'flower' for a river or stream, or 'Webster' for a spider, or 'butter' for a ram or goat. But today such well-used terms, and scores of others in similar vein, have become part of a complex crossword language that has evolved over the years. For the early compiler the dictionary was a storehouse still to be ransacked; the solution to almost every clue was one that nobody had used before, and he had not encountered the bogeys of repetition, unconscious imitation or staleness.

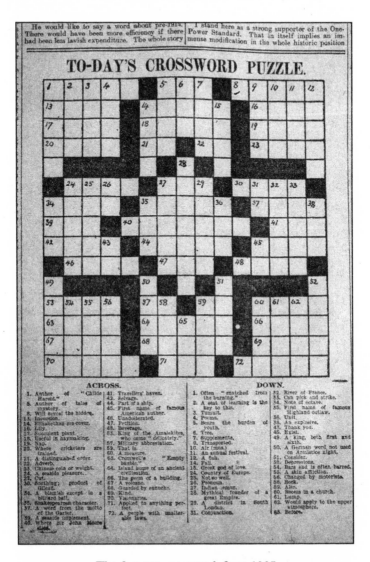

The first ever crossword, from 1925

30 July 1925

ACROSS

1 Author of *Childe Harold* (5)
5 Author of tales of mystery (3)
8 Will reveal the hidden (1-4)
13 Incursion (4)
14 Elizabethan sea-rover (5)
16 Lily (4)
17 Succulent plant (4)
18 Useful in haymaking (5)
19 Nap (4)
20 Where cricketers are trained (4)
21 A distinguished order (2)
22 Adverb (2)
23 Chinese coin or weight (4)
25 A seaside pleasure (4)
28 Cut (3)
30 Soothing: product of Gilead (4)
34 A blemish except in a billiard ball (4)
35 Shakespearian character (5)
37 A word from the motto of the Garter (4)
39 A seaside implement (3)
40 Where Sir John Moore died (7)
41 Travellers' haven (3)
42 Selvage (4)
44 Part of a ship (5)
45 First name of famous American author (4)
46 Unadulterated (4)
47 Petition (3)
48 Beverage (4)
53 King of the Amalekites, who came 'delicately' (4)
57 Military abbreviation (12)
59 That is (2)

60 A measure (4)
63 Cromwell's 'Empty bauble' (4)
64 Island home of an ancient civilisation (5)
66 The germ of a building (4)
67 A volcano (4)
68 Guarded by eunuchs (5)
69 Kind (4)
70 Visionaries (5)
71 Applied to anything perfect (3)
72 A people with unalterable laws (5)

DOWN

1 Often 'snatched from the burning' (5)
2 A seat of learning is the key to this (4)
3 Tumult (4)
4 Poems (4)
5 Bears the burden of youth (4)
6 Tree (3)
7 Supplements (4)
9 Transported (4)
10 Air (mus.) (4)
11 An annual festival (4)
12 A fish (5)
14 Fall (4)
15 Greek god of love (4)
24 Mythical founder of a great Empire (7)
25 Country of Europe (5)
26 Not so well (5)
27 Pronoun (2)
28 Indian lemur (5)
29 A district in South London (5)
31 Conjunction (2)

First Telegraph crossword printed

32 River of France (5)

33 Can pick and strike (5)

34 Note of octave (3)

35 First name of famous Highland outlaw (3)

36 Unit (3)

38 An explosive (3)

43 Thank you (2)

45 Exist (2)

49 A king, both first and sixth (5)

50 A German word not used on Armistice night (4)

51 Consider (4)

52 Depressions (5)

54 Bars and is often barred (4)

55 A skin affliction (4)

56 Changed by motorists (4)

58 Rock (4)

59 Also (4)

60 Recess in a church (4)

61 Lump (4)

62 Would apply to the upper atmosphere (4)

65 Before (3)

3 May 1926

ACROSS

1 Two things are this if they can take each other's place (15)
9 News (7)
11 A name of the blue titmouse (7)
13 Lubricates (7)
14 Quarter of an acre (4)
16 One of what you are reading (4)
17 Inclines (5)
19 In this the unlucky trout is put (5)
20 Stagger (4)
21 The best kind of tree for a hedge on a farm (5)
22 A Latin word often met with a legal 'decree' (4)
23 Set of persons working together (4)
25 Long-nosed American mammal (5)
27 Approach (4)
29 Spectacle (5)
30 Boredom (5)
31 Remainder (4)
32 Stand for an important branch of the army (4)
33 Russian vehicles with teams of three horses abreast (7)
37 Reflexive pronoun (7)
38 First (7)
39 In a cowardly manner (15)

DOWN

1 A linguist is needed for this job (15)
2 A frog but not a frog (7)
3 Part of a ladder (4)
4 Shown by short skirts (4)
5 Used in writing (4)
6 Ostriches of Australia (4)
7 Microscopic rod-like organisms (7)
8 We speak thus when we say 'last sleep' for 'death' (15)
10 Eighteenth President of the USA (5)
12 Be taught (5)
15 Determine the boundary of (7)
16 A perfect equestrian was probably the origin of this mythical monster (7)
18 Young branch (5)

General Strike starts

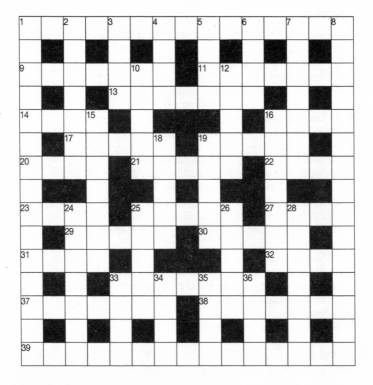

19 Skeleton packing case (5)
24 Takes for granted (7)
25 Boor (5)
26 Famous billiard player (5)
28 Evelyn's is one famous example of these (7)
33 Small freshwater duck (4)
34 Eighth century King of Mercia (4)
35 Quaint bird of New Zealand (4)
36 A farmers' alternative to making hay (4)

21 May 1927

Lindenberg's first solo flight of the Atlantic

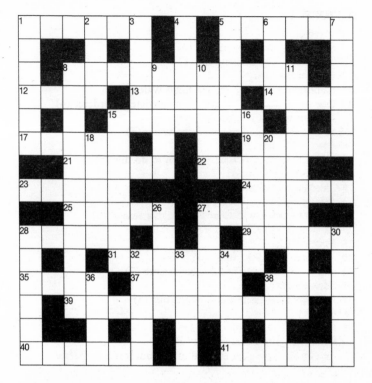

15 Agitation (7)
16 A ship had better be this than 37 (7)
18 Correct (5)
20 This will nearly fill a quart bottle (5)
26 Proportion (5)
27 Character in *The Rivals* (5)
28 The cause of an eclipse (6)
30 Book of the *Old Testament* (6)
32 Vacant (5)
33 Internal (5)
34 Order (5)
36 Incline (4)
38 Insect (4)

7 May 1928

ACROSS

1 Adventurers of old (though grammarians might prefer a different plural) (6,7)
10 'A plover' (anag.) (7)
11 One of the USA (7)
12 'Thou rebel damsel, do me the favour of tying this turban,' quoth the knight (hidden) (6)
15 Determine (6)
16 Room (7)
17 Part of the body (4)
18 At Molokai a settlement was provided for lepers by Father Damien (hidden) (4)
19 African ruminant (7)
20 Loosen (4)
22 Book of the *New Testament* (4)
24 'Cheer it' (anag.) (7)
26 Drink (6)
27 City of Spain (6)
30 Make of motor-cycle that would have been popular in ancient Rome (7)
31 Employ (7)
32 There is a pleasing superstition about these bones (5,8)

DOWN

2 Points for a yachtsman (7)
3 Pace (6)
4 What you are looking at now (4)
5 Prevailing (4)
6 The belle hopes her beau is this (6)
7 Weed (7)
8 A bar to marriage (13)
9 These give varied views (13)
13 However clever this man is he is generally at sea (7)
14 This fish lived under an alias (7)
15 'Fur ties' (anag.) (7)
21 Refuse (7)
23 British hills (7)
24 Tool (6)
25 Part of a wall (6)

Parliament passes Women's Suffrage Bill

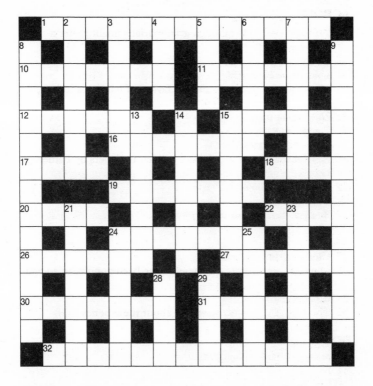

28 Sharpen (4)
29 Great French writer (4)

28 October 1929

ACROSS

1 Battle that gives its name to a 16 (9)
9 Swiss town (6)
10 'Be thou a —— of health or goblin damn'd . . . Thou comest in such a questionable shape that I will speak to thee' (Shakespeare) (6)
11 Pull (4)
12 Province or wine of Spain (6)
13 Kind of dog (9)
15 A constituent of gruel (3)
16 Geometrical shape (6)
19 The game of table tennis is similar to ping-pong (hidden) (3)
21 Presenting difficulties (7)
22 Implement (7)
24 He may earn the name of fool who kicks against the pricks (hidden) (3)
26 Hinder (6)
29 A little bit of Cambridge (3)
31 A 'rat', a 'pig' and a 'man' together will make a bird (9)
32 'The —— we delight in physics pain' (Shakespeare) (6)
34 Musical instrument (4)
35 Members of a South American race that gave their name to a sea (6)
36 Dressing (6)
37 Island in the South Atlantic (9)

DOWN

2 Weapon (6)
3 Enthusiasm (6)
4 The kind of refuse that is dear to a sow (6)
5 The tale (anag.) (7)
6 Spanish old master (9)
7 Ladies' quarters in the East (6)
8 Indoor game (9)
9 Don't get stuck by this vessel upside down (3)
14 This fold is popular with the young (4)
17 Waver (9)
18 Kind of car (9)
19 May follow the name of a professional man (3)

Collapse of the New York Stock Exchange

20 Ship of a kind (3)

23 One of the deer family (4)

25 Simple (7)

27 'And this our life, exempt from —— haunt, finds tongues in trees . . . and good in everything' (Shakespeare) (6)

28 Nursery (6)

29 Great river of Asia (6)

30 Cane (6)

33 The heart of a brute (3)

24 May 1930

ACROSS

3 Of many a cocktail gin is this (5)
8 A fine material made of its end (6)
9 Is this three (6)
10 Just pop in with fifty more (6)
11 Spanish dance (8)
12 A time of literature (3)
13 English shire (6)
14 Kind of biscuit (8)
17 One should not let a hero come back to his native town thus (7)
19 The man who lets his opportunities go this way may be this later (7)
23 Valueless, though containing a valuable card (8)
27 One might expect this bird to be able to perform mysteries (6)
29 You will find this seed in a pear, for example (3)
30 A stammerer might get practice in demanding this in his salad (8)
31 China from China (6)
32 From haste take it and serve raw or boiled (6)
33 Many think we could do with more of this and less of Law in our courts (6)
34 Class of bird (5)

DOWN

1 Florid in style (6)
2 English town (8)
3 Not one of the fair (8)
4 Top, apparently the top man among the breakers (7)
5 Verse (6)
6 Say (6)
7 The event of 1665 (6)
13 Without this the skilled solver will be able to write this here (5)
15 This helps to make wheels go round (3)
16 You will find this berry easy to grow in your garden (free hint) (5)
18 A toy mentioned in these clues (3)
20 Cambridge College (8)

Amy Johnson flies from England to Australia

21 Flower (8)
22 A Belgian town you see enclosed in a tree (7)
24 One of the twelve tribes (6)
25 Name of a weapon that sounds like our Tom (6)
26 A beginning of life (6)
28 'Do I sit?' (anag.) (6)

3 March 1931

1 This kind of majesty being evil naturally has a dark heart (7)
5 This popular machine generally does without its first two letters in ordinary life (7)
9 Hungarian musical composer (5)
10 What the wise town-dweller likes to do for a holiday (9)
11 Pigeon or poet (5)
12 Title of a Shakespearean play (9)
14 Port of Idaho (3)
15 Beastly-headed proportion (5)
16 A joint shows a wager about a danger (7)
19 Poetic commands (7)
22 The kind of song popular with an Angling Society (5)
24 Colour (3)
25 Italian hero (9)
29 Unnecessary instruction to a miserly housekeeper (5)
30 'Trill, dame' (anag.) (9)
31 Stone that would seem to be suitable for a portal (5)
32 To perfection (7)
33 Part of a horse that appears to shrink (7)

DOWN

1 Suitable chemical for the person in 1 *across* (7)
2 A great game they no doubt play sometimes in Bryant and May's (4,5)
3 Both famous and infamous (9)
4 Liqueur (7)
5 Stage property for a witch (5)
6 Name famous in the history of India (5)
7 This American mammal looks as if it might figure in an indent for clothing (5)
8 Mountain that is always in hybrid language (7)
13 Exclude (3)
17 Perpetual (9)
18 What bird's name might a mother-cat invoke? (9)
19 Make of car that often appears in the racing world (7)
20 Meal (3)
21 Kind of tumour (7)

'Star Spangled Banner' adopted by US

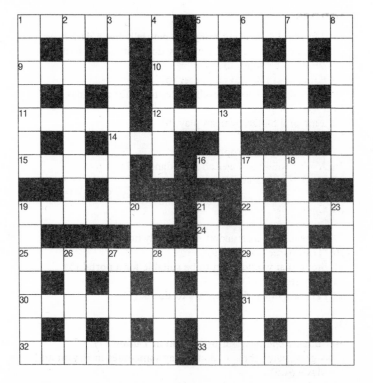

23 'The —— Nymph with wonder saw, a whisker first and then a claw . . . she stretch'd' (Gray) (7)

26 Thread, bird or official (5)

27 An official of ceremonies (5)

28 The unprofessional (5)

19 March 1932

ACROSS

1 Guard work this; or is it an Irishman going home from a wake? (10)
6 This was once an idol and afterwards eaten by its worshippers (4)
10 A fabulous being (5)
11 Official who can always show the substance of the matter (9)
12 Disgusting (8)
13 Part of a ship where the cables emerge (5)
15 It is possible to get money from the pit's end (7)
17 This describes some two-year-old, perhaps (7)
19 Scottish artist (7)
21 'She mewed to every watery god some speedy aid to send; no —— came, no Nereid stirred' (Gray) (7)
22 This land is in Africa (5)
24 Suburb where metal is found (8)
27 Imperious (9)
28 Punch, probably (5)
29 'See what a —— the envious Casca made' (*Julius Caesar*) (4)
30 These give pleasure to the 17 (10)

DOWN

1 Boat or bet (4)
2 Famous fighting vessel of former days (9)
3 Pigment (5)
4 Famous cricketer (7)
5 'Slight', says the dictionary, rather misleadingly (7)
7 Take the first letter from a farmer's implement to make this weapon (5)
8 Patient (10)
9 Plant with a poisonous head (8)
14 'Rest, O Roman' (anag.) (10)
16 Rivals (8)
18 Opera title (9)
20 What you want here is necessary (7)
21 Badness in the dry is worse than mischief (7)
23 'We hustle the jungle bears on as Alice dares not' (hidden) (5)
25 Some Oriental potentate (5)
26 From these little fellows one would expect 21 down (4)

Sydney Harbour Bridge opens

14 July 1933

ACROSS

1 Work of a railway engineer or of a gardener (7)
5 Disadvantage (7)
9 A red wine (5)
10 Keepsake (7)
11 See nothing for a game (3)
12 Cook uses this for flavouring (5)
13 Apparently unique kind of type (9)
16 A kind of crest in Japan (3)
17 The author of the *Marseillaise* (5)
18 The very end is an awkward situation (9)
20 Blunt advice to a child about good manners (9)
24 Foundation (5)
27 Paradoxically only one bit of driftwood (3)
28 Old man that looks like a valuable racehorse (9)
32 This inhabitant of the sea would still be in good health if you cut off its head (5)
33 Tune (3)
34 A gentle revolutionary is related (7)
35 Due (5)
36 Book of the *Old Testament* (7)
37 Heraldic position (7)

DOWN

1 Humorous (7)
2 A change from the outside (7)
3 This is severe in a man that might be a Pope (9)
4 'No anger' (anag.) (7)
5 A spirit from the French world (5)
6 A deadly serpent (5)
7 Lady of rank in the East (5)
8 The movement in this kind of truck seems rather unsafe (7)
14 You will find this is a European capital (3)
15 Creature that can be found in 37 (3)
19 Plenty of space for the person (5,4)
20 Hide not the porcine race (7)
21 A lady (3)
22 A line of topped elms (3)
23 Vessel in which cooking may be done (7)

German parties other than Nazis forbidden

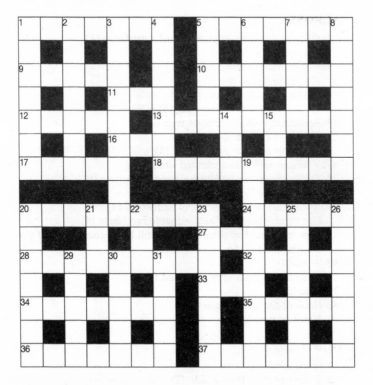

25 'It's a man' (anag.) (7)
26 Dexterity that sounds slender (7)
29 Country of Asia (5)
30 No joyful music (5)
31 Great river of Asia (5)

19 August 1934

ACROSS

1 Where even the mildest committee member often says 'hang it' (5,7)

8 He might well have been brought up in the ruling fashion (7)

9 Vegetable finally useful at a pinch (7)

11 Language (7)

12 The man who wants to be this is probably a stout fellow (7)

13 Where there is but one example of this there will be a host (5)

14 He has his counterpart in commerce (9)

16 If you can hand out what's coming to him, it's a gift (9)

19 One of grave predilections (5)

21 A flourish from the trumpet (7)

23 In this the turnover is continuous (7)

24 Town of Surrey (7)

25 If he had played golf he would have made light of bad lies (7)

26 Wherein many a Christian martyr died (12)

DOWN

1 A good answer (7)

2 A rosy protagonist (7)

3 A handy form of spectacle (9)

4 Many simians geographically prominent (5)

5 Not very wide-awake pets (7)

6 You want some hint, of course, but I will give you as little as possible (7)

7 When this is introduced into the house a certain coolness may be apparent (12)

10 One of the head examiners (12)

15 If your first idea for this is wrong, try every other (9)

17 The middle is on a tree but strengthen the whole (7)

18 Royal and Ancient gentleman who preferred pyramid to golf (7)

19 Brave (7)

20 7 is useful for preserving, this opening is needed (7)

22 Deflect (5)

36

Hitler becomes Germany's head of state

1935–44

By the mid-1930s the cryptic crossword had become more sophisticated. Improved patterns, many of which are still used today, totally banished the American concept of groups of white squares. This allowed compilers far more flexibility and the puzzles gradually increased in complexity.

In the decade in which Hitler rose to power and the world was engulfed in war it is easy to forget that other more mundane events occurred. In 1937 J. M. Barrie died and *The Daily Telegraph* introduced the daily Quick Crossword as an additional feature in the puzzle corner – it immediately claimed a following of its own. In this decade Sir Jack Hobbs was still scoring centuries at cricket, Persia was renamed Iran and Edward VIII abdicated, but naturally it is the Second World War that dominated this period.

With the outbreak of war, Britain's changed economic circumstances were reflected almost immediately in the size and appearance of all newspapers. A paper shortage was inevitable and a bare two weeks after war was declared, on Tuesday, 5 September, *The Daily Tele-*

graph dispensed with solution diagrams. As an economy measure the crossword's solutions were printed in typescript instead – a practice that lasted for seven years, during which the overall size of the paper shrank year by year. By 1941 the paper had only six pages, but the crossword was *always* printed – smaller in area but not in content – on the back page to which it had been moved the previous year and has remained ever since.

Two famous episodes of crossword history occurred during these ten years, both concerning *The Daily Telegraph*'s puzzle and a connection with codes. The first relates to a crossword competition whose participants were contacted as potential code-breakers for Bletchley Park – the hub of the War Office's code-breaking efforts. And the other was the mysterious appearance of D-Day code words in the crossword.

The competition – solving a *Telegraph* crossword against the clock – was the result of a flurry of letters in the paper (following the appearance of the 5,000th puzzle) about how quickly the *Telegraph* cryptic crossword could be solved (the sort of letters that still grace the correspondence pages of the paper from time to time). The claim provoked W. A. J. Gavin, owner in the early part of the century of the journal *Vanity Fair*, to issue a challenge – published in the *Telegraph*'s letters column on 3 December 1941:

> I challenge your correspondent who claims to have solved the crossword of the previous week in six minutes to make good his claim by solving one of your prize crossword puzzles in double that time.

If he succeeds in doing so you are authorised to send the enclosed £100 Bank of England note [about £2,500 in today's money] to the Eccentric Club Minesweepers' Fund.

My challenge, which allows 12 minutes for a solution, extends to all of your correspondents who claim to do your puzzles in such incredibly short periods of time.

The editor invited readers who wished to accept the challenge to send in their names. In due course, on Saturday, 10 January 1942, twenty-five competitors assembled in the newsroom of *The Daily Telegraph* in Fleet Street. One of them, L. Ashton Sly, of Salisbury, Wiltshire, recalled the event some years later:

Conditions were not really conducive to concentration and quick solving of a crossword puzzle. We were at separate desks – reminding us of our long-past school examinations – each with two sharpened pencils (B and HB), a sheet of virgin blotting-paper, a new india rubber, and a dictionary (little use in such limited time). In front of us sat *The Daily Telegraph* officials with stop-watches; photographers were round the walls. Twelve envelopes were produced, each containing a set of the puzzles due to be published on one of the days during the coming fortnight, and one of us chose at random a date during that period.

The first competitor to complete the puzzle was Vere Chance, of Orpington, Kent. He did so in 6 minutes

3.5 seconds, but, alas, he misspelt one of the words in his haste and so was disqualified. The actual winner was F. H. W. Hawes, of Dagenham, Essex, who took 7 minutes 57.5 seconds. He was presented with a cigarette lighter by Arthur E. Watson, the then editor, on behalf of the newspaper's proprietors. Three more contestants beat the 12-minute deadline and a further four more hands went up in the 13th minute. So the Eccentric Club Minesweepers' Fund got its £100.

An interesting sequel to the event was that the War Office got in touch with all who accepted the challenge with a view to training them as cryptographers for enemy code-breaking work at Bletchley Park.

The second more famous incident involved the D-Day landings of 1944.

The nub of the affair was five words that appeared as solutions in *The Daily Telegraph* crossword in the fortnight or so preceding D-Day. Each of these words was a top-secret classified code word connected with the landings themselves. *The Daily Telegraph* crosswords printed in late May and early June 1944, which included the five D-Day code words, were all compiled by one man, Leonard Dawe, the paper's senior compiler and a contributor of crosswords to *The Daily Telegraph* since they first appeared. He was by now the headmaster of the Strand School, which had been evacuated to Effingham in Surrey. Dawe was staying with his brother-in-law, Peter Sanders, who occupied a very high position in the Admiralty. Thus, one can understand why MI5 was deeply suspicious of the appearance of code words in the *Telegraph* puzzle.

It is, however, entertaining to speculate how MI5 discovered these code words in the puzzles; was a bigwig in the Admiralty an avid crossword solver who noticed with alarm these top-secret words and got in touch with MI5? Was a small department of MI5 devoted to solving the crosswords in all the nation's papers in case Nazi spies were using them to pass messages? We will never know. All that we can be sure of is that Dawe, a man of impeccable character, convinced MI5 that the appearance of these code words in his puzzles was pure coincidence – he was not a German spy passing information to his masters through the pages of the *Telegraph*. However, some boys who were taught by him mischievously chose to remember his Prussian haircut, his admiration of things German and his visits to Germany, but no one seriously thought him a spy.

Dawe was obviously shaken by the experience. He later recalled of MI5:

> They turned me inside-out and collected naval intelligence and grilled my brother-in-law. They went to Bury St Edmunds, where my colleague Melville Jones was living, and put him through the works. But they eventually decided not to shoot us after all!

'The Case of the Coded Crosswords' has proved a constant fascination since it occurred and has been mentioned, not necessarily accurately, in numerous films, plays and books. The true story came to light in the mid-1980s from one Ronald French, who had been a 14-year-old pupil at the Strand School in 1944. According to French, it was Dawe's occasional practice on wet afternoons to invite favoured pupils into his study where, as a mental exercise, he would encourage them to fill in the blank puzzle grids he was working on. French claimed that D-Day code words were common knowledge in the area – where many Canadian and American service men were billeted awaiting the invasion – and that boys living locally were familiar with them, though unaware of their meaning. French was fascinated by the prospect of the invasion and kept notebooks containing the information he obtained. The code words duly found their way into Dawe's grids. French recalled:

> Soon after D-Day, Dawe sent for me and asked me point blank where I had got the words from. I told him all I knew and he asked to see my notebooks. He was horrified and said that the books must be burned at once. He confiscated them . . . He then gave me a very stern lecture about national security and made me swear on the Bible that I would tell no one about the matter. I have kept that oath until now.

What we will never know is whether Dawe pacified MI5 by telling them of French's knowledge or whether he misled the officers, believing it his duty to protect a naive young pupil.

The Daily Telegraph

LONDON, WEDNESDAY, JANUARY 16, 1935.   LONDON LATE EDITION   ONE PENNY

Daily Telegraph
All the Real News

SIR A. KEITH'S
DEFENCE OF
DARWINISM

Front page from 1935

15 September 1935

ACROSS

1 This old weapon suggests a great reduction in the number of workers (12)
8 Chief (7)
9 This hotel name sounds as if it is secluded (7)
12 This bow never shoots arrows (4)
13 A great lake (5)
14 Flower or feminine name (4)
17 Kindred (7)
18 Relative (7)
19 A shelled creature (7)
22 A resin product (7)
24 Precious stone (4)
25 A seed that may retard human progress (5)
26 Aid to Oriental beauty (4)
29 This boat is all in a place for sale (7)
31 To fall into line (7)
32 Does this bit of the bird make one laugh? (12)

DOWN

1 Trembling, as Royalty (7)
2 Biblical host (4)
3 This religious rite seems a matter of a certain weight (7)
4 A bird in stone is useful in a boat (7)
5 This traveller's payment has a sad sound (4)
6 Tree (3)
7 Insufficient food this, certainly unsuitable for the Long Parliament (5,7)
10 Drug useful in medicine (5)
11 Troops for rapid movement, but not necessarily from the RAF (6,6)
15 Cambridge college (5)
20 A tropical forest plant (5)
21 A place of main attraction (7)
22 A wind (7)
23 The sentry to give a warning (7)
27 Imputation (4)
28 A modern drawback (4)
30 A musical sound, but it sounds rather doubtful (3)

Germany's Nuremberg Laws outlaw Jews

2 November 1936

ACROSS

7 Islands of the Pacific (9)
8 Short work for a lawyer (5)
10 He should be a tactful person (8)
11 'Unship' (anag.) (6)
12 A modern 10 (4)
13 Is it a dentist's work that makes a person sing this? (8)
16 Scarcely compos mentis (4)
18 Wicked epithet for an atheist (7)
20 Obviously an outer garment (7)
22 A feline (4)
24 'A fuss about Nell being upset' is your clue (8)
26 Suitable prize for the shoemaker who won the slow-cycling race (4)
29 Force (6)
30 Old port (8)
31 Vegetable (5)
32 Guarantee of self-confidence (9)

DOWN

1 Sounds like a golfing colonel but is part of a railway car (5)
2 When a card-player decides to go for a nap, he lets this drop (6)
3 Hereon a vessel is almost capsizing (8)
4 Emblem of women, not only of spinsters (7)
5 Majesty (8)
6 Accomplished in more than one way (9)
9 Precious stone (4)
14 Part of a tomato (4)
15 Flower that may appear on the stage at Christmas time (9)
17 Serpents as a literary afterthought (4)
19 An old-fashioned sweet (8)
21 Brave (8)
23 Vain advice about the pepper to the Duchess's cook in Wonderland (7)
25 Sheep found in the West Indies (4)
27 This modern aid to advertising is made of slang and nothing more (6)
28 No, this tool is a single one (5)

BBC start the first regular television service

6 May 1937

ACROSS

1 In this country there is, inter alia, a ban of some sort (7)
5 A dupe, but is not without natural weapons (7)
9 Feature of today that limits clear vision (7)
10 Fish to keep around the fleet (7)
11 An official badge, perhaps (7)
15 Part of a rifle (7)
19 He who lags in the race should make this (5)
21 This stone could at one time have destroyed its end (6)
22 Any departure from this is bound to be lowering (6)
23 Not unconsciously situated (5)
24 Dance (6)
25 A recent great loss to literature (6)
26 An Eastern shelter has not become lower (5)
29 A wrong note may be this (7)
32 A striking cause of note issue (7)
36 Offence not without boast (7)
37 Spring helps her to live (7)
38 A saw of sorts (7)
39 A bird colony started by a brave man (7)

DOWN

1 With him a part is everything (5)
2 Part of the minstrel band, or other body (5)
3 One of the obscure results of world revolution (5)
4 The lady of three articles (6)
5 The ugly duckling (6)
6 There appears more than one (5)
7 This is rarely a hanging matter with the modern girl (5)
8 Bird (5)
12 He examines pupils (7)
13 He knows a good thing when he meets it (7)
14 This building is never without warmth (7)
16 She was fair but false (7)
17 Apparently a very tough spell (7)
18 One finds this right in a hockey team (7)
20 His Pa was the making of this warrior (5)
27 In having done it well, this is well (6)
28 The spirit of the North (6)

52

Airship Hindenburg destroyed by explosion

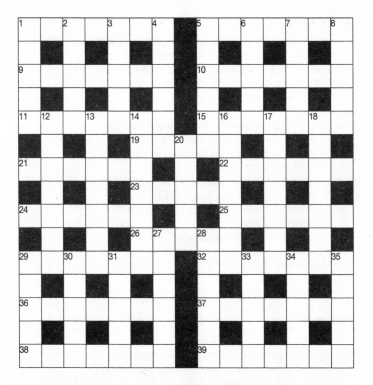

29 This emerges from pursuit without it (5)
30 Forbidding association of thanks and derision (5)
31 English novelist (5)
33 Have this and the crossword any connection? (5)
34 It needs a beak to do this properly (5)
35 Metaphorically out of practice (5)

30 September 1938

ACROSS

1 He often takes the pledge but does not always keep it (10)
9 Ignoble part of America's favourite game (4)
10 A commercial transporter of excellent breeding (5,5)
11 Pick from the rag (6)
12 Save from the dance (5)
15 Epithet for the exit of the sensitive-nosed from its end (5)
18 The reason why some people want to fly (5)
19 There's a bad joke in it – wash out! (7)
20 An aim does not make sense (5)
21 An aid gives fair result (5)
22 The beginning of this town should get on swimmingly with the end (7)
23 It may seem near endless to a watchman (5)
24 Dwelling for deposit? (5)
26 This river finishes at right angles to the direction it starts in (5)
29 Animal that shows hesitating acknowledgment of ownership (6)
31 What borrowers are apt to do is a close thing (5,3,2)
32 It's fine in the Sahara (4)
33 The willing horse may be this, and so may the weak-willed (10)

DOWN

2 A German title that runs in England (4)
3 He may not have a shirt to his back, but he likes it (6)
4 Velocities that seem to go up and up (5)
5 It has a shady population (5)
6 Turn wrath to a distance (5)
7 Accounts item that includes two parts of the body (4,2,4)
8 Mark down but disapprove if I go (10)
13 Vegetable in recess tends to calm (7)
14 Some young buck may provide it (7)
15 Half of this dish was hung high (3,3,4)
16 Part of West Africa (10)
17 Reformed as yet (5)
18 Where the organist put his foot down (5)
25 Considered in the heart (6)

Chamberlain's 'Peace in our time' speech

26 A bout (3,2)
27 Harden (5)
28 From there comes the spirit (5)
30 Monster made by soldiers to be under a king (4)

3 September 1939

ACROSS

5 What a noise! (6)

8 In this no company is permissible (8)

9 A famous lover of oysters (6)

10 The middle of this departed period was an eyesore (4,4)

11 This may be related to anyone (4)

14 Menacing reports may be all about him as he carries others (8,5)

19 Epithet for a people mostly very much in the public eye (5)

22 When Turkish it is sweet (7)

23 A bit of horse gear (5)

25 A party game (7,6)

31 Bird (4)

33 This means a change for footballers, but it makes them fail (4,4)

34 Where to put water when the house is this (2,4)

35 Black usually (8)

36 To escape him a hare must be out of form, yet in good form (6)

DOWN

1 Thus trimming is a comfort (6)

2 Of the highest excellence (6)

3 To get the least adulterated one must mix up with what's left (6)

4 The lack of many on earth (6)

5 Where Honolulu is (6)

6 It is meant for the rest, but the rest was finally disturbed – the lobster mixture was responsible! (7)

7 Santa Claus unwisely shows it the wrong way (5)

12 Irish firebrands upset over some article – and to some tune too! (4)

13 One would often like to forget what one has said, but this may make it all come back to one (4)

15 The backbone of South America (5)

16 This is middling painful (5)

17 Concerning the coster's girl there is something quite above her station (5)

18 Might give useful shelter in an air raid (5)

War declared on Germany

20 Put away from one direction to another (4)
21 After hooking this kind of fish, one has to play it of course (4)
24 Shrewd, but not in the best sense (7)
26 A little devil starts to put obstacles in the way (6)
27 Can one ever feel this abroad? (2,4)
28 It is not part of a hue and cry oddly enough (6)
29 While this one might commit murder, but only in play (6)
30 One wanderer with the end of many (6)
32 She ran with phonetical ease (5)

26 May 1940

ACROSS

1 Of course the watches aboard as well as ashore have to be this (9)
6 Was this early discoverer a sleeping sailor? (5)
9 No whisper upsets him (9)
10 Fruit (5)
11 Often a way through (3)
12 Set apart (9)
15 Expensive sort of stone to make a way in (5)
16 Perhaps a precious stone (5)
19 Name well known in the world of cricket (5)
21 Opposed to the downs (3)
22 This introduces an exception or a contrast (3)
23 Social rank (5)
24 After an accident it is often desirable to get a this on (5)
26 Province of India (5)
27 Obviously one who may give orders (9)
31 Bird of no high origin (3)
32 Only one American author (5)
33 Change to tall men (9)
35 Freshly coloured like a certain river fish (5)
36 This game suggests some whisky made like beer (9)

DOWN

1 Used by billiard players when they are playing oddly enough (5)
2 Preliminary to the fall of the hammer (5)
3 Unrestrained (5)
4 Part of 8 (3)
5 Lament (5)
6 Used doubtless for planning out round trips (9)
7 'Blue? Agree!' (anag.) (9)
8 One of the United States (9)
13 Old port (3)
14 Mountain made famous by Dumas (5)
16 No, his work is not at the labour exchange (9)
17 Oppose not without some position of defence (9)
18 A sort of discount known in Irish bargains (9)
20 Fresh or salt-water fish (5)

Allies' evacuation of Dunkirk begins

25 A piece of furniture (3)
27 Two letters as one do not agree (5)
28 'The rusty curb of old father —— the law' (*Henry IV, Part I*) (5)
29 You may have found this lasted some time in a good welt of a shoe (5)
30 This may permit rotation in only one direction (5)
34 Would this motion of the sea suit a cutter? (3)

7 December 1941

ACROSS

1 The sun's gift to give thy girls a change (5,4)
6 Three-dimensional (5)
9 This soldier protects a fellow (9)
10 A boy be around for the cutter (5)
11 Many travelling for a map line (7)
12 Part of the war RA ignore (7)
13 Not to the fore at sea (3)
14 This may put a girl in the shade (7)
17 This reckless fellow had about nothing to the middle (7)
19 You should see him race in correct form, it's simply fabulous (7)
22 Prophet in source of strains has facial defect (7)
24 Any forbidding change (3)
25 See that your black-out material has it (7)
26 To give a conceited person a good blowing up may this him, oddly enough (7)
29 What's his strong point? Never mind! (5)
30 'Ales at bar' (anag.) (9)
31 It may get bloodstained, but is easily made clean (5)
32 Atlas and Cain in infernal confusion (9)

DOWN

1 One can reason with it (5)
2 There's a growing demand for itself beheaded to swell it (5)
3 It's rather boring from the outside (7)
4 He is claimed as a leader by the modern without fashion (7)
5 Brown will mark the man who takes it (3-4)
6 Many a man's wife might feel a bit scratchy about the bare part of this show (7)
7 Imaginary standard of perfection (4-5)
8 Purified, or destroyed (7,2)
14 The films are this sort of entertainment (9)
15 Disaster comes to a whole people at last (9)
16 End of 11 (3)
18 It's backward in flavour (3)
20 Convenient form in which to record one's pet lies (7)
21 Familiar street cry, or part of it (3,4)
22 The AFS have an attachment for it (7)

Japanese attack Pearl Harbor

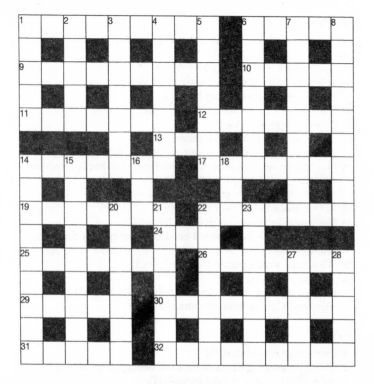

23 Think of a tune, but don't sing it! (7)
27 It can come to be a frolic (5)
28 Add your name to the list (5)

10 June 1942

1 Girl Communist from Cornwall? (7)
5 A smack with it would silence a rook, of course (7)
9 The flower of a vessel in flower (7)
10 Nice place for more sickly doctor in Sicily (7)
11 Not how to make tart, oddly enough (7)
15 A good tip? (7)
19 It may be given for scrap (5)
21 Remove the tee to get off; a sweet effect! (6)
22 No small number (6)
23 Just short of share is turned to air (5)
24 Flippant name for projected entertainment (6)
25 A real sticker in medical circles (6)
26 There has been a wealth of speculation as to its whereabouts (5)
29 It might be administered to the suffering via 25 (7)
32 The answer to this is by no means obvious (7)
36 Bad Australians took to it (3,4)
37 Describes the habits of a duck (7)
38 Unchristian enough to cook a bird (7)
39 More than a giant, but so fairylike was she (7)

DOWN

1 Army transport is a puzzle! (5)
2 For a slacker there can be only one end (5)
3 Given an excessive tip, apparently (5)
4 Man in colour is kindly disposed (6)
5 Architectural feature like inverted first half (6)
6 He works on engines (5)
7 Vessel to run into violently (5)
8 As they grow up they grow down (5)
12 This 17 describes many a jumper (7)
13 All washed out, but the face is plain (7)
14 Writer who might have made me snore (7)
16 Charitable cupboard? (7)
17 There may be more than one to suit (7)
18 Beheading this would make itself (7)
20 It might easily be a drain on one's estate (5)
27 Bird (6)

Nazis wipe out Lidice, Czechoslovakia

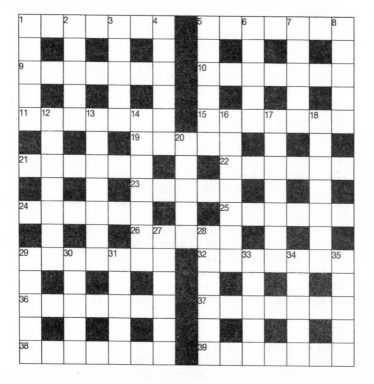

28 The effects of it are mutually striking (6)
29 This bone comes from an ox (5)
30 Musical address of spot in Turkey (5)
31 The longer one lives the further it recedes (5)
33 Short and broad (5)
34 Your last meal was this, of course (5)
35 An exotic flowering shrub (5)

23 January 1943

ACROSS

1 A luxury for those with money to burn? (7)
5 The number of letters in it may vary (7)
9 He wears no rose-tinted spectacles, though is later converted (7)
10 There's art in it, of course, and often satire as well (7)
11 Not what they print American financial news on; yet! (9)
12 Rare spirits from the East (5)
13 She's pleasing when she loses her heart (5)
15 To this cognition a window-cleaner may usefully aspire (9)
17 'Dad inside' (anag.) (9)
19 Property varies in this value (5)
22 It is skinny, stringy, and has a twang (5)
23 All over the place, but turned colour in decline (9)
25 Cow (7)
26 An officer being guilty of it doesn't make it a sin of commission (7)
27 It is passing strange to the motorist abroad (7)
28 Use the wiles of Delilah, but pay attention in part (7)

DOWN

1 Just a sideline incident in sport (5-2)
2 The touching type (7)
3 In off a saint leaves no flabby result (5)
4 What the disgruntled batsman found the firm umpire to be (9)
5 Running helper (5)
6 He couldn't stay, apparently (9)
7 Epithet for the boy who had a good tanning? (7)
8 The ingénue turned out to be no poser (7)
14 Turn from one state of matter to another (9)
16 Ancient and modern (3,3,3)
17 It would be very questionable to confer any dignity on a debtor's promises (7)
18 Much the same as 8 or 4 (7)
20 Where to look for 6 (4-3)
21 He may get what's left as a right (7)
23 Would hardly describe a well prepared plot (5)
24 Flying symbol of more than one land (5)

Eighth Army enters Tripoli

1 June 1944

ACROSS

1 'Lid on slang' (anag.) (but is all 15 *across* so pure in speech?) (4,6)

8 Doing nothing because there's nothing doing possibly (4)

10 The kind of constitution that laughs at doctors of the Goebbels type! (10)

11 Our supposed portion in 1940, but we never tumbled to it . . . (4)

12 . . . though coming to the this of it (4)

15 Where the work of the architect stands very high (3,4)

18 The girl who went into her own reflections very amusingly (5)

19 You must be plumb right! (5)

20 Just a note (5)

21 Got in wrongly to the bar (5)

22 Would this problem be a sitter to an artist? (5)

23 A joint affair (5)

24 Not a forbidding hue (5)

25 She is in an ancient city (official!) (5)

26 Of Eastern origin, but serious (7)

30 Cast a skin (4)

33 Points in favour of some players? (4)

34 A submarine should be, of course (10)

35 He gets his wings on false pretences (4)

36 Where to look for Maud's boyfriend? (6,4)

DOWN

2 Sign of appeal to men (4)

3 Cause of the hidden hand? (5)

4 Like a bear with a sore head (5)

5 He may be like the curate's egg, good in parts (5)

6 Outcast agents of fickle chance (4)

7 Flower one might well salute (4)

9 End of a term for losing cohesion (8,2)

10 Those working in it are quite sunk in their work (6,4)

13 It may be seen at the front at feeding time (5-5)

14 See printer for an adventure (10)

15 Britannia and he hold to the same thing (7)

16 Sphere of 15 *down* (5)

17 An exclusive notice (4,3)

Another D-Day code word in the crossword

20 The root of smokers' pleasures (5)
27 It comes from the rates – blooming scandal! (5)
28 Choice of directions of tongue (5)
29 Was an arm, or might support one (5)
31 No good man will live up to it (4)
32 Shoot to spot (4)
33 Finished! (4)

1945–54

No one is going to argue too much with the statement that the ten years between 1945 and 1954 were fairly grey. It was an age of utility furniture, rationing and nationalization with two brief bright blips – the Festival of Britain and the coronation of Queen Elizabeth II.

In these years of gloomy anti-climax following the end of the Second World War crossword puzzles continued to provide an important avenue of escape. One addict wrote to the paper in 1947 suggesting that the then Ministry of Food should introduce a few pages of puzzles into the ration books 'to while away the time while queuing'. Quite a few puzzles would have been needed because rationing did not end completely until 1954 – almost a decade after the war had ended.

It was not until 1946 that the cryptic crossword's solution grid reappeared – hardly a world-shattering event in a year that saw the first sentences passed at the Nuremberg trials, the first A-bomb tests at Bikini Island and the Bank of England nationalized. But it mattered to *The Daily Telegraph*'s readers, some of whom had been reduced to using magnifying glasses in order to check their crossword answers.

In fact, it is interesting to speculate how today's crossword solvers would have managed those puzzles from 50 or more years ago. Of course, you will be tackling some in the next few pages, but the clues will be nicely spaced out and in an easy-to-read typeface. Imagine them squashed into a space ten centimetres wide by seven deep – not easy on the eyes by any stretch of the imagination!

But crossword solvers from 50 years ago were made of sterner stuff: in 1948 one fan wrote: 'At last! After searching for many years, I have found a square containing all 26 letters of the alphabet!' One wonders whether it was Dawe or Jones who inaugurated that first 'alphabet' puzzle – a constraint that is now quite common among some compilers who, occasionally, like to make life hard for themselves.

With the return to the routine of a peace-time working life, the position of the puzzle on the back page assumed an extra importance for solvers. The letters column contained virtual dissertations on the technical niceties of how to fold the paper for the best working conditions on the train or at the office.

One attribute that would surprise modern-day solvers is the frequency of quotations as clues in crosswords of this period:

Clue: 'Hear you this Triton of the ——s?'
    (*Coriolanus*) (6)
Solution: *Minnow*

Clue: 'There is a pleasure in poetic pains which
—— poets know' (Cowper) (4)
Solution: *Only*

These now are rare, but at that time a quotation clue such as these might crop up every week – an occurrence that many modern solvers would find totally unacceptable. But this was an age when the written and spoken word reigned supreme. Television was in a delayed adolescence, having been taken off the air in 1939, not to return until 1946 and then only in black and white for a limited number of hours a day. For example, on Tuesday, 16 May 1950 this would have been your selection on the sole BBC channel (no independent, satellite or cable TV yet):

10 a.m.–12 Demonstration film – running on sets placed in shop windows, showing potential TV buyers the delightful programmes on offer. All interspersed with the famous test card.

3 p.m. *Shop at Home* – a demonstration of domestic products made from aluminium.

3.30 p.m. *Tapisserie d'Art* – a French film telling the story of tapestry.

3.45–4 p.m. *Andy Pandy* – programme for young children.

8 p.m. *Tomorrow We Live* – a film on the German occupation of a French port.

9.25 p.m. *Ask for the Moon* – Arthur C. Clarke on why man could colonize the moon.

9.55–10.10 p.m. News (sound only).

No wonder cryptic crosswords were so popular – with or without quotation clues!

It was around this time that the shadowy figure of an editor for the *Telegraph* crossword first makes an appearance. Dawe and Jones were still providing all the puzzles and their crosswords had reached a high level of sophistication: 'Skilful French direction' (6), solution: *Adroit*, from puzzle No. 8366 in September 1952 would not be ashamed to show its face in a 2005 crossword. But such a level of cryptic nicety meant that every word in the clue had to be accurate – no misprints were allowed. And it is at this stage that the names of Margery Williams and Margaret Binstead first make an appearance, carefully shepherding the puzzle into the paper with every full stop and semi-colon in place.

In 1951 Winston Churchill became prime minister once more, after a general election when the Conservatives were brought back to office following a post-war Labour government. However, plans for the Festival of Britain were already well under way. It brought a little colour into people's lives and an opportunity to look to the future rather than back to the war. Staged on the south bank of the Thames, it is most remembered for the Skylon, thrusting upwards to the sky – 'a tall thin structure with no visible means of support, rather like the British economy' as one pundit of the time put it – and the Dome of Discovery, though its most lasting monument has been the Festival Hall.

The Festival was a quasi-government project and civil servants, like compilers, were developing a language all their own. In the post-war years there was an outbreak of officialese that could verge on the incomprehensible. The only similarity between a good cryptic clue and official gobbledygook (as it came to be called) is that both challenge the reader to make sense of it, the main difference being that the good clue does it with wit! This nice difference was overlooked by the recorder at an Old Bailey hearing when he exclaimed, as a civil servant in the Ministry of Works was giving evidence, 'It all sounds like a crossword puzzle!' The witness spoke of 'incremental dates' (for when a pay increase was due), 'by the usual internal delivery system to his in-tray' (a messenger put a note on his desk), 'assimilation of the increased salary scales' (general pay rises) and 'the pre-assimilation conditioned hours' (hours previously worked). That was in 1954. Both languages have evolved further since then.

Indeed, the terminology used in the court which so baffled the reporter seems almost commonplace when compared to the language of today's workplace. Phrases invented in marketing and advertising, for example, have slipped into common speech, not to mention phrases arriving with the advent of technology and computers. A plethora of acronyms and invented words have been occasioned by 'txting' and emails. (How long before the first 'txt' crswrd pzle?) Further, politicians and spin doctors continuously spout complex soundbites to confuse the public or fudge the fact they have nothing to say. But most importantly, words that were used without the smallest twitch of an eyebrow could potentially provoke law suits for their racial, sexual or homophobic connotations. See for example clue 15 on 4 April 1949. But racial intolerance and innuendo became par for the course in the 1950s and to erase the traces of them would be to tamper not only with crossword history, but with history itself. How on earth will we understand why people behave as they do now if we don't take on board what happened in the past?

No. 5,792

ACROSS

1 A shot that falls short is not thus satisfactory (four words—2, 2, 5, 4)
9 Town of Germany (5)
10 "Call In a home" (anag.) (11)
11 The Derby winner to start a branch of mathematics (5)
12 Tree used in the building of the Temple (5)
15 Town to go down in times of drought (5)
17 Drink upset in 10 across (3)
18 To get this fabulous lady just ponder (4)
19 Ecclesiastical assembly (5)
22 Its sole work is to produce some effect (5)
23 Not obsolete (two words—2, 3)
24 Battle of the last Great War (5)
26 One probably these represented at a 19 across (4)
27 The start of 35 across (it's given you) (3)
28 This worker is as good as five in the R.N. (5)
30 The way in which a tasty lemon might come in useful (5)
33 An overworked word nowadays for 'rate' (5)
35 This gives vagueness to place or number (11)
36 Lightweight of the animal world (5)
37 The credit for a joint thus perfectly cooked should go to the turnspit (four words—4, 2, 1, 4)

DOWN

2 This meal would be bit by bit (5)
3 Red Indian on the Missouri (5)
4 Wine (4)
5 No small deer (5)
6 He wrote "A thing of beauty is a joy for ever" (5)
7 By sticking to one's work (11)
8 A mere jumble of words (11)
12 At any rate a writer of music should have this to offer importunate creditors (11)
13 Kind of absentmindedness (11)
14 Gathering in which all take part (5)
15 This continental river might easily become a drain (5)
16 Sign of the Zodiac (3)
20 Displeasing (3)
21 One of the worldly wealthy (5)
25 Stands for the control of the lower Thames (3)
28 Well-known refusal given to the lad (5)
29 Edge (6)
31 Fish that resists your getting him his tail (5)
32 Afterwards (5)
34 This term for a European of sorts seems to be 500 years old (4)

QUICK CROSSWORD

ACROSS

3 Sudden speed
8 Fish
9 In good time
10 Last
11 Like
13 Dish
14 Fruit
16 Wandered away
19 Engrossed
21 Ulcer
22 Transgressors
24 Despatch
26 Part of church
28 Annihilate
29 Dwells
30 Journal
31 Might
32 Peruses

DOWN

1 Delicate
4 Demand
4 Compute
5 Garner
6 Aerees
7 Idleness
10 Attaches
11 Disdain
12 Complaint
15 Bears
17 English poet
18 Prepared
20 Drinker
23 Food
24 Condescend
25 New
27 Weary
26 Defunct

Printed and Published by THE DAILY TELEGRAPH Ltd., 135, Fleet-street, London, E.C.4, and at Withy Grove, Manchester, 4.

Crossword from 22 May 1944.

The solution to *3 down*, 'Red Indian on the Missouri' (5), was a code word from the D-Day landings, OMAHA.

15 October 1945

ACROSS

1 For holiday attire in Norfolk? (10)
9 The watering-can needs it for watering it (4)
10 'Atom as ruin' (anag.) (victims treated here?) (10)
11 Having been given a depressed area (6)
12 One thing Hitler never conquered; he didn't come across it (7)
15 He doesn't object to breaking in, but to disciplining (7)
16 It may need a ruler to keep it straight (5)
17 There are blue and white varieties of it (4)
18 One of things that are laid down on board (4)
19 Interval for father to employ (5)
21 Pass over without a break, this has to do with it (7)
22 It needs crack experts to tackle it (4,3)
24 This, for the moment, is you (6)
27 Berlin is, and is not (2,3,5)
28 To be supplied very shortly, we fear! (4)
29 Promptness is the duty of a punitive force (10)

DOWN

2 Half a century from 16, on paper (4)
3 No ancient battle would have resulted from this river reversing its course (6)
4 One of those utterers of poor notes . . . (7)
5 . . . whom one might well this and never miss (4)
6 Indulge two annoying mannerisms in a tedious way (7)
7 You may see him at a State opening of Parliament (10)
8 Sensitive in the extreme, perhaps because of inexperience (10)
12 Plot that ends in crime on the main (10)
13 Not a salt-water 8 (4,6)
14 Quite allowable, and to be trusted even heartless (5)
15 Lending becoming colour to a bride (5)
19 Shows no turn in a parson for an innkeeper (7)
20 The centre of this part of London is like a number (4,3)
23 Posted as an undemocratic ruler (6)
25 End of 23 comes to rest (4)
26 A small circle as numbers go (4)

78

Former Premier of Vichy France executed

18 April 1946

ACROSS

1 May mean nothing but implies duty (5)
4 He shines at his work (9)
9 Knowledge or a large branch of it (7)
10 Not suitable regimen for a high feast (3,4)
11 She was back in the All England netball team (4)
12 Not a strong kind of basket (5)
13 Will this cause a competitor to scratch? (4)
16 Not always a desirable quality in a brief (7)
17 On examination, unless plucked, has a place over the pupils (7)
19 Depending on repeated untruths (7)
22 The officer to put a stop to the Spanish (7)
24 Where usually to find plenty of cars still (4)
25 More than one 28 always in France (5)
26 Scottish island (4)
29 A small bird (7)
30 Overcast (7)
31 Get under logs for this weed (9)
32 Modern fabric (5)

DOWN

1 Consumption here has brought death to the natives (6,3)
2 He's pretty sure to be some gaffer (7)
3 Very small part of a plant in your garden (4)
4 'O, —— not —— the moon' said Juliet (5,2)
5 Pluto, if up to date (3,4)
6 It is more likely to be in the saloon than here that the fiddles will be seen (4)
7 He may fly from danger without being to blame (7)
8 Vessel (5)
14 Is it after five! (5)
15 Oxford college (5)
18 A capital part, it sounds, to find William in his own room (9)
20 Scottish school where the main job comes first (7)
21 Foundations of 31 (7)
22 One of the lynx family (7)
23 'Key land' (anag.) (7)
24 Tine (5)

The League of Nations dissolves

27 Design (4)
28 Not exactly straightforward trip (4)

3 June 1947

ACROSS

1 Capital place for a drink in very warm surroundings (6)
4 The weapon to supply a sticky end (8)
9 Should peers speak in this manner? (6)
10 Occupation for two principals and four seconds (8)
12 Wrongly said to be a place of honour (4)
13 A good housewife doesn't this when she can make a stew of it (5)
14 16 this is bit by bit (4)
17 Utter destruction (5,3,4)
20 Remembering about a gathering (12)
23 'A soldier full of strange oaths and bearded like the —— ' (*As You Like It*) (4)
24 This kind of room is not necessarily Greek (5)
25 A prick from this flower may become its anagram (4)
28 A danger to bathers (8)
29 A vegetarian might or might not eat this vegetable (6)
30 A long time (8)
31 Cold and wet like a shellfish (6)

DOWN

1 Describes the view of a ship near the horizon (4,4)
2 The fortification of a London street (8)
3 Depend (4)
5 Legal term, not the price asked in the shop (7,5)
6 Masculine form of 14 (4)
7 Some hard worker (6)
8 Treat mainly in royal fashion (6)
11 Can one see this fish only when the sun shines in a shower? (7,5)
15 'Then felt I like some watcher of the —— ' (Keats) (5)
16 Only a part (see 14) (5)
18 'I mark log' (anag.) (8)
19 On the move, not necessarily by tube (5,3)
21 A neat tree (6)
22 Yet this path doesn't lead to the altar (6)
26 English river cricket term (4)
27 The time of year when Adam ate the apple (4)

Partition of India announced

5 July 1948

ACROSS

1 A heap of stuff about an underground play? (4,4)
5 Settle about the upper part, and cease whatever you are doing! (4,2)
9 The road to celestial well-being? (5,3)
10 Something one can bite on concerning olden times (6)
11 A necessary process before the manufacture of 16 (8)
12 Playgoers may have seen *Oliver Twist*, but hardly this! (6)
14 She is never truly at home in the tropics (5,5)
18 This chink has not yet seen the light, apparently (4,6)
22 The only bird that is allowed about the pub? (6)
23 What this produces will help in bridge-raising (5,3)
24 British bird of note to wait inside (6)
25 One of the few places where people move with an eye to their carriage (8)
26 Not a permanent colour, it could be erased (6)
27 Plant also known as the king's spear (8)

DOWN

1 This plant can be presented in many species (6)
2 Many deceptions florally presented (6)
3 An animal that is at first not very forthcoming (6)
4 'A last pinch' (anag.) (for you, of course, not at you) (7,3)
6 Part of the regalia (3,5)
7 Wherein every man is a man of leisure (8)
8 Motto for 4? (2,3,3)
13 This and 16 are from a well-known and paradoxically captivating quotation (5,5)
15 Judging by this fellow paganism and procrastination go together (8)
16 See 13 (4,4)
17 Taken as agreeable, as far as the present is concerned (8)
19 To say our northern neighbours are this is sure to wound them slightly (6)
20 English town within which a varied tour is possible (6)
21 Mostly a foreign fruit, all on the saddle-tree? (6)

Introduction of the National Health Service

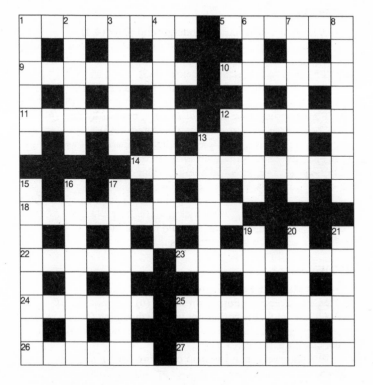

4 April 1949

ACROSS

 1 The birthplace of many vessels (9)
 8 Instinctively, perhaps (13)
11 He might become a Cardinal one day (4)
12 It's a rum sort of drink (5)
13 Mole that cannot grow without help (4)
16 It comes from the Nore (7)
17 'And not by —— windows only, when daylight comes, comes in the light' (Clough) (7)
18 He might help the marksman to get a clearer sight (7)
20 Superior kind of groyne (3,4)
21 Stone valued no doubt by John Peel (4)
22 One of those that helped to name Sheridan's play perhaps (5)
23 Mohammedan spirits (4)
26 But one wouldn't use this system for counting the casualties (4,9)
27 Easily, in jockey's metaphor (5,4)

DOWN

 2 To get this, the cracksman uses the reverse of it (4)
 3 There's nothing on besides a pull for the soldier (7)
 4 Axis of which the berry is decorative (7)
 5 Sounds like the weight of a little drink (4)
 6 More properly hookahs (6-7)
 7 They are not entire repetitions but only initial ones (13)
 9 Not the committee in charge of a Devon river (4-5)
10 The worm that apparently could make a permanent mark on a fish (9)
14 The account heading that shows I owe (5)
15 The part of Asia from which Sambo's master came back (5)
19 The tapering part usually (4,3)
20 Cereals are usually before being threshed (7)
24 Just think of something and that is what you want (4)
25 This don is surely the tallest of them all (4)

North Atlantic Treaty signed

24 February 1950

ACROSS

1 Many a ship goes daily from this river (5)
4 A person of such a character should suitably be sent to Coventry (9)
9 Stonehenge may be of such origin (7)
11 Food that has a dear sound? (7)
12 Possible disaster left when one is taken from 2 (4)
13 It has eight gills but doesn't breathe through them (5)
14 It was just a small part of the Indian Mutiny (4)
17 The tale of *Peter Piper* perhaps (6-7)
19 Describes some outstanding event in one's life (13)
21 A constituent of Germanic languages (4)
22 Yet this sound from the nestling would sound dear to the mother bird (5)
23 Arabian spirits (4)
26 This sort of fire burns in metal (7)
27 It may be seen on a modern florin (7)
28 The run needed to make the score complete (9)
29 They may form a cascade (5)

DOWN

1 Officially descriptive of the Malay States (9)
2 The island for a social meeting (7)
3 Leather (4)
5 'Ten tame divers' (anag.) (13)
6 It is finished when the musical part has left 4 (4)
7 More unpleasant form of stainer (7)
8 He might have been called a buck in Regency days (5)
10 A legal term, not the cash shop price (7-6)
15 The old Third Foot Regiment (5)
16 The condition to put into words (5)
18 They have swarms of admirers (5,4)
19 Ignorant as even a learned person may be (7)
20 Port where 21 *down* is held in honour (7)
21 Though just a sailor in bed, famous as an explorer (5)
24 Inclination out of order in 27 (4)
25 African, not necessarily among the rabble (4)

Labour wins election with slim majority

3 May 1951

ACROSS

1 'Eat bits only' (anag.) (11)
9 The look of a heartless 17 (4)
10 Annoying and even making it worse (11)
11 It may form a cup, a warning or a musical instrument (4)
14 Where letters have some value (7)
17 Any 4 by this man should have an elevating influence (5)
18 A trial impression, literary or artistic (5)
19 Rational people seldom take action without it (5)
20 Mountainous part of Europe (5)
21 He appears in a halo serving to mark a saint (5)
22 Strictly correct to enforce (5)
23 Large town of France (5)
24 It may sharpen and be sharpened (5)
25 'His —— shows the force of temporal power' (*The Merchant of Venice*) (7)
29 Symbol of servitude (4)
32 'I renew rivet' (anag.) (11)
33 This helps to show the age of a tree (4)
34 Some enterprise with perhaps grave ending (11)

DOWN

2 Slang trousers (or plus fours?) (4)
3 'All our pomp of yesterday is one with Nineveh and —— '
  (Kipling) (4)
4 Something new in the way of literature (5)
5 If a man has to make this payment he does get it back at the
  end (5)
6 The owners of this vessel have more than one (5)
7 The form that love took in Leander's heart (4-7)
8 Electric gadget desirable in a fairy's wand (11)
12 These railwaymen do not have more waiting to do than others
  (11)
13 Able to see but perhaps turning a blind eye (11)
14 A heart that is this shows a third person (7)
15 Not a desirable sort of 24 (5)
16 Simian (7)
19 Many talk nonsense to beg (5)
26 Sounds like one of the big guns of the clerical world (5)

Festival of Britain opens

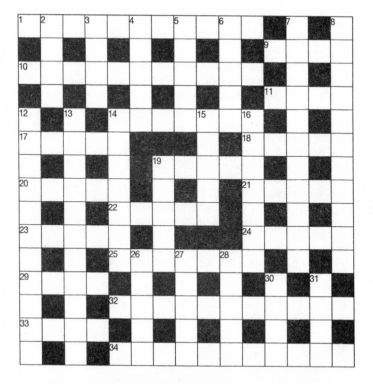

27 This work gets paid by results (5)
28 Join together five in a broken row (5)
30 The part of the vessel to make pretty (4)
31 Opposite of 15, sad as it may sound (4)

6 February 1952

ACROSS

1 Part of Greater London to extend in breadth and trade back inside (9)

9 A hymn writer, but not of the modern school (6)

10 Regal weight in Surrey (8)

11 This room is an apparently low class place, only for those who have no class at the moment (6)

12 A writer using unfair copy in the middle (6)

14 March sees its rise and fall (4)

15 The part of TV transmission one can shut one's eyes to (5)

16 Two articles in degree bear fruit (6)

18 An entertaining collaborator with 33 (7)

21 A Bantu like a girl about a tree (7)

24 Points to a game of squash? (4,2)

26 He could have made a kind of beer, but his work was in bars anyhow (5)

30 Space (4)

31 Rousing advice one can hardly close one's eyes to (6)

32 A hero of Gaelic legend (6)

33 See 18 (8)

34 It can hardly be classified as fact or fiction (6)

35 Self and Red Dean certainly made no bee-line (9)

DOWN

2 Unreasonable state that I'd begin chilly about zero (6)

3 Open architectural feature, half wood (6)

4 Dog a prophet about an abstainer (6)

5 Give one of the commoner type a lift up (7)

6 There's a good deal in a vegetable that reminds one of this game (6)

7 A mineral that gives point to a writer (8)

8 The last misfortune that can befall the exile from home is getting less and less (5,4)

11 Nutty artist responsible for some striking death scenes? (5)

13 This town curtailed will continue to grow (4)

17 Battle as a suitable site for a spirit game? (9)

19 Not associated with any company, but one's honour is included (8)

20 The town that a tombstone may have (5)

King George VI dies in his sleep

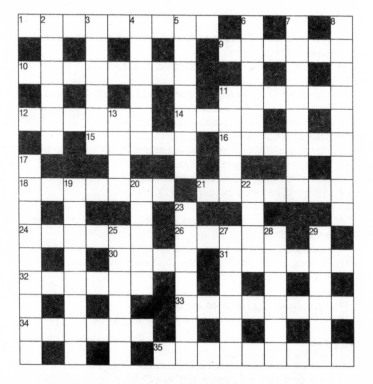

22 Poetical wood for a playwright (4)
23 Lands end seem confused (7)
25 Planetary father of Saturn (6)
27 There's bitterness on this amount (6)
28 Some troops long for plunder (6)
29 Quite composed, though capable of being teased (6)

2 June 1953

ACROSS

1 Sometimes it's quite a good wheeze to play it (10)
6 Change a fish to a berry (4)
10 This will stagger you, though the middle's a winner (5)
11 It's a great help in cutting things fine (9)
12 This comes from the coals, and is good pickled (8)
13 The short distance that may get one time (5)
15 Don't trust him, he may do you a bad turn (7)
17 Bright remark mostly concerning two animals (7)
19 Denoting a gland from third half of 29 (7)
21 They need sunshine, though they may be beyond it! (3,4)
22 Combine or gain, I'm certainly lacking (5)
24 One of those blooming climbers (8)
27 Understand how to add about her in turn (9)
28 As in general it warrants occupation (5)
29 It travels a lot, but is always kept on a string (2-2)
30 Upon it depends how great is the tax on one's resources (10)

DOWN

1 A refreshing change of face (4)
2 Her children are patently protected (9)
3 One thing at least that never tires of the daily round (5)
4 Nimble chap who ought to be able to hold his liquor (7)
5 Making a knot in it may often remind a man of his birthday (7)
7 What is this may be a rattler (5)
8 Disposition that is by no means odd (4,6)
9 What you can't find now, you'll have to make up for (4,4)
14 Still capable of showing that Tito's Aryan (10)
16 Soundly beaten, being partly only a lightweight (8)
18 Where there's life there's no call to this (9)
20 The lady who was game at the last (7)
21 The rocker responsible for revolution (7)
23 Nomad the reverse of pig-headed (5)
25 A world-embracing volume (5)
26 And, finally, something to make you smile (4)

Millions cheer as Queen is crowned

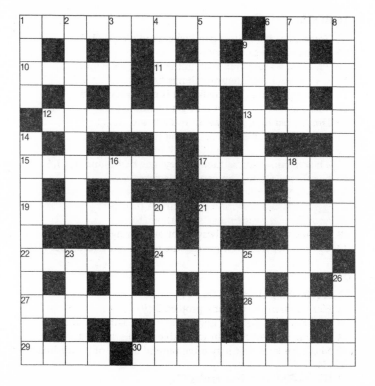

6 May 1954

ACROSS

1 It is cultivated, but not in a natural way (10)

9 May be the sort of boom that helps shipping (4)

10 Qualification is a topping thing with skill (10)

11 Wash out what is allowed in a river (6)

12 Headgear, brown, sailors for the use of (7)

15 Highly strung, no doubt, from the actions of 29 (7)

16 One spot in Africa that moves slowly about nothing (5)

17 There are two kinds of this, and it is painful to strike the wrong one (4)

18 A hole surrounded by string, often (4)

19 Was very sad from credit being curtailed (5)

21 One of the more pleasant results from the use of a cane, but let care be taken in the making (7)

22 Deck for a costume dance? (5,2)

24 This includes the kind of fuel that might be used to heat it up (6)

27 'Tinkers had' (anag.) (then they did care a tinker's cuss!) (4,6)

28 His name should not occur to you all at once! (4)

29 The press on the war path? (5,5)

DOWN

2 The lion's share of what comes to one's ears (4)

3 A man of mystery is about to fashion figures (6)

4 The start of the autograph hunter's prize (7)

5 Title I show up in the flag (4)

6 Put down times to do with shipping (3-4)

7 In no position to put one's thoughts into words (10)

8 Mutual bond that has the aims at heart (10)

12 Citizens ask them everything, and they will even tell you what a child does in arithmetical preparation (10)

13 As high as one is prepared to bid? (5,5)

14 The mother of a lovely and precious daughter (5)

15 All cows have this, and many have not fulfilled their obligations (5)

19 The centre of this flower is a veritable shelter for animal life (7)

20 No doubt this has given way to the motorski, or whatever the word is! (7)

Bannister breaks four-minute mile

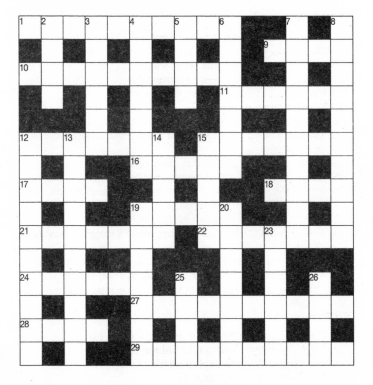

23 Not a shanty, but what may waft it (3,3)
25 Anti-aircraft weapons tucked up for the night (4)
26 This away, travelling, doesn't pay! (4)

1955–64

This ten-year period saw an explosion of activity throughout the world – political, social and intellectual revolutions were the order of the day. But among the world-shattering events of the late 1950s – the Suez Crisis, the birth of the Warsaw Pact, the fledgling independence of a host of African countries, the launch of the first Sputnik satellite and the advent of Fidel Castro in Cuba – news of domestic import jostled for a place on the *Telegraph*'s front page: 'Standard Men Vote to Continue Strike' was the headline on 1 May 1956. The story concerned 11,000 Standard Motor Company workers continuing their unofficial stoppage in protest against the company's move to lay off men.

On 5 March 1957 one front-page story concerned a wrangle in the House of Commons. The then prime minister, Mr Macmillan, was defending Sir David Eccles, President of the Board of Trade, against a Socialist charge that he had "prematurely disclosed a Budget intention".' Ah, such innocent times . . . And in 1959 there was the delightful front-page tale of the 'Dooley gang', 'a group of boys and girls aged between six and 14 years', who foiled a five-man ambush of a mail van in Paddington by calling 999 and reporting the criminals in action. Dare one say that in 2005 in certain areas of this realm a daring five-man ambush might be *perpetrated* by a group of boys and girls aged between six and 14 years.

Things were also on the move in the world of *Telegraph* crosswords. In the mid-1950s Melville Jones retired making way for a new compiler, Douglas St P. Barnard, who had been an intelligence officer with the Australian army during the Second World War. He was to compile crosswords for the *Telegraph* for more than 40 years, as well as setting tests for Mensa, creating a myriad of mathematical puzzles, writing books, taking an active role in local Cheltenham politics and amassing a charming collection of porcelain. Indeed, the elegance of his porcelain collection could be said to match the elegance of his crossword clues.

In 1958 *The Daily Telegraph* printed its 10,000th crossword – compiled by the indefatigable Leonard Dawe. Margery Williams, who was editing the crosswords at that time, wrote an article for the paper analysing the popularity of the puzzles as she saw it. She referred to the vast mail that came from crossword puzzle addicts:

> 'The puzzles are too easy: does the compiler think he is pitting himself against the second form of St Dorothy's . . .'

'The puzzles are too difficult: does the editor think that a chap has nothing else to do all day but grapple with his wretched puzzles?'

'There are too many anagrams . . .'

'There are too few anagrams . . .'

'. . . too many allusions: is the writer expected to carry the *Encyclopaedia Britannica* to the office and back with him?'

'There are too many quotations: does the editor imagine that his public has Shakespeare by heart?'

Margaret Binstead who worked with Mrs Williams and was *The Daily Telegraph*'s crossword editor for almost 20 years confessed to getting more or less the same complaints; and I, who succeeded her in 1977, also get those same complaints around 15,000 crosswords and 47 years later . . .

In 1961, Leonard Dawe wrote a short article in the paper explaining how to go about compiling a crossword. Having selected a pattern, the would-be compiler was enjoined to:

Select a word that you think will suit. Pencil in (lightly!) only the letters that will stand at the crossroads (or key spaces). Now consider interlocking words that these letters will fit. You will probably find several. Again, pencil in the additional letters given by the selected words at vacant key spaces. As you proceed, the choice, naturally, becomes more restricted, and the use of an india rubber and fresh ideas may be called for . . .'

Nicely put, Mr Dawe, and still true.

In that same year the US-backed fiasco of the Bay of Pigs invasion of Cuba took place, as did Yuri Gagarin's pioneering space flight. But once again quirky stories insinuated themselves onto the paper's front page. On Wednesday, 3 May 1961 a top story carried the three-tier headline (three-tier headlines were much favoured at this period):

DETECTIVE ON EAVESDROP CHARGES

WIRES IN DUCHESS OF AGYLL'S CAR

IMMUNITY FOR HEARSE DRIVER

Now, who could resist reading that one involving the Duchess of Argyll, a New York private eye masquerading as a car-hire service manager, a bugged Cadillac and a part-time-chauffeur-cum-full-time-hearse-driver? And there it is nestling between a picture of the queen at a state ball and one of King Hussein of Jordan with his British fiancée, Antoinette Gardiner. Eat your heart out, *Hello!* magazine.

Two years later, Leonard Dawe died and Alan Cash, a man of the Black Country, stepped into his shoes. He gave up the day-job (teaching English) three years later and became the *Telegraph*'s chief compiler, supplying three puzzles a week (as well as puzzles for the *Scotsman* and other smaller journals). He had left school at 16 and studied for a London University external degree in English, history and German in his spare time. He had his first puzzle published in the *Daily Mirror* (1931) while he was still a schoolboy and had later supplied the (now defunct) *News Chronicle* on a regular basis – he once told me how he used to compile his crosswords by hurricane lamp in his tent in the North African desert while on active service during the Second World War. He compiled almost 3,000 puzzles for *The Daily Telegraph* and in 1988 he died in harness, just as his predecessor had done.

In the year that Alan Cash joined the *Telegraph*'s team President J. F. Kennedy was assassinated and De Gaulle vetoed Britain's entry into the European Economic Community. The following year China exploded its first H-bomb and Harold Wilson became prime minister.

CEASE-FIRE MOVE GAINS MOMENTUM

SIGNS OF CHANGING VIEWS IN U.S. & CHINA

SIR A. EDEN WORKING ON FORMOSA ISSUE

PEKING INVITES RELATIVES TO SEE GAOLED AIRMEN

BY OUR DIPLOMATIC CORRESPONDENT

2 ISSUES FOR WASHINGTON

CHIANG LOSES KEY ISLAND

CHIANG: AIRMEN HIT 70 SHIPS

MR. G. WESTON'S £2,500,000 BID FOR ABC TEASHOPS

2 DARTMOOR MEN CAUGHT IN 1 a.m. CHASE

LORRY CRASH AT BRIDGE: BOTH INJURED

DAILY TELEGRAPH REPORTER

PLEA TO MOVE U.S. HOSPITAL IN ENGLAND

W. INDIES TOUR

BANK GUARD DISAPPEARS

PREMIER RECEIVES RAIL PAY REPORT

LATE NEWS

PURCHASE TAX ON FURS CUT FROM MONDAY

REDUCTION IN RATE ON PAPER GOODS

MORE ARRIVE FROM JAMAICA

LOSS REST FOR GILBERT HARDING

SHIP ON SCILLY ROCKS DURING DENSE FOG

FLARES GUIDE LIFEBOAT IN RESCUE OF CREW

DAILY TELEGRAPH REPORTER

NIGHT FOG HALTS ALL AIR SERVICES

2 CLIMB 325ft CLIFF IN DARK

ORPINGTON WIN

MORE ARE LIKES TO-DAY

14 May 1955

ACROSS

1 The management of this may call for skilful casting and playing (7-3)
9 A journey into antiquity? (4)
10 This is conducted by the one examining body (4-6)
11 State that is extant, or gone, perhaps (6)
12 Given a broken tail, this place would be quite necessary (5)
15 The things he is responsible for are often penned in (5)
18 Back waters run fast here (5)
19 The way in inside is nothing out of the ordinary run (7)
20 Ancient Ethiopia (5)
21 A quality in management that propels things along the road to success (5)
22 Chain article well known in Canada (7)
23 Speak well of what was once a backward lot (5)
24 Place for 26 *across* to lodge is a sound return to us (5)
26 When they arrive in a body one may be excused for feeling hot and bothered (5)
29 A destructive creature of small beginnings but largely bad (6)
31 Lot's fate may well recall him to mind (10)
32 Its attachment to 1 is well known (4)
33 Brokenly tensed, with a heart of water, and pessimistic (10)

DOWN

2 Figure of personal action with a number (4)
3 A rising feature of current importance (3,3)
4 It may precipitate a tight situation that is inescapable (5)
5 Examples of 18 *across* that are assiduously collected (5)
6 If this bad one is upset he inclines to be less vigilant about me (5)
7 'Get out, Enid' (anag.) (or else say something!) (6-4)
8 Danger was responsible for the beginning of these troops (10)
13 A great deal may be gleaned from it at times (7)
14 Bright remark of one animal to another upset (7)
15 The pest that created the Roman wreck (6-4)
16 Soured by beer in muddled meed (10)
17 Just the place for a lark in Africa (5)
18 A great victory to have been carried away by (5)
25 Hotly pressed after being washed out (6)

Warsaw Pact signed by Soviet Union

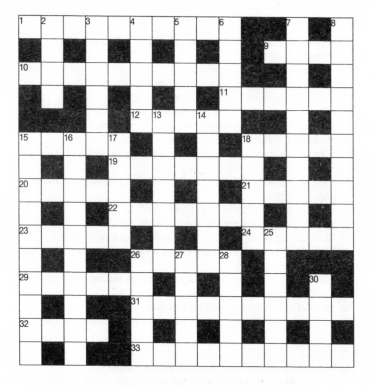

26 Part of the body that is mostly earth (5)
27 Sways gently at the water's edge, often (5)
28 Sounds like a cunning business in Ireland! (5)
30 In very cutting form (4)

26 July 1956

ACROSS

1 Container figures in place of addresses (3,7)

9 Hardly an innocent sort of parcel (4)

10 He may urge you to buy cigarettes, being glad himself of free puffs! (10)

11 Even this and a ton would not manage all of it (4)

12 Hard work for the motorist and the tennis-player (5)

15 If he is good then his master will be well suited (5)

18 A letter showing a few in debt to ten times as many (5)

19 Certainly something to raise the wrath of a puritan (7)

20 One of those old dug-outs not much good in a row? (5)

21 The hiding they once gave led eventually to a plaguey result (5)

22 As exciting as an alarm clock? (7)

23 Classic date singular between poles (5)

24 To make a mistake or to make a mistake (5)

25 Speculators who horn in on new concerns (5)

28 A minute opening which takes over to study closely (4)

31 Confused signal in part of London from the USA (4,6)

32 It plays its part in toasting (4)

33 Alone I'd get to what autocrats do not practise (10)

DOWN

2 The race is hardly open when these are on (4)

3 A joyous time for a man's name either way (4)

4 Its hands betray what is consumed (5)

5 It enables a painter to work with it curtailed (5)

6 The place of antiquity in cunning is hardly pleasant in nature (5)

7 Untilled plant growing up as an animal (6,4)

8 Just the stuff to get fires re-lit and land re-stocked (10)

13 Bill of airman tally (7)

14 To the true philanthropist this is an action of no interest (7)

15 Empty intrigue that some might think to build on (6,4)

16 Does this cupboard contain material for the newspapers? (5-5)

17 Merely rows, but apparently succeed in making knots (5)

18 There's a measure of work in a border of this sort (5)

25 As green as turning to youth? (5)

Egypt seizes the Suez Canal

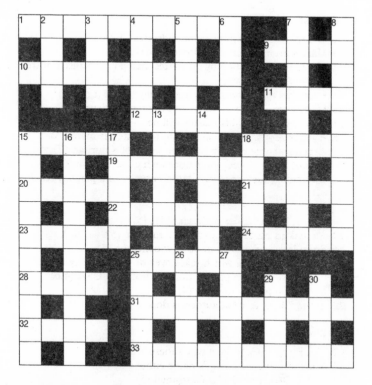

26 If you can do this to a mistake you are lucky (5)
27 The painful end of a honey gatherer (5)
29 Hardly a sound abode for a good musician! (4)
30 Reverse the work of 17? (4)

19 January 1957

ACROSS

1 This beheaded could be the man who hit his toe with it! (7)
5 Even those who don't have money to burn buy it (7)
9 Accommodation, providing food and the rest (3,3,9)
10 Poachers' victims, often (4)
11 As decoration for a special occasion it has its points (5)
12 Sharp's the word if the ship is lost (4)
15 Their occupation may be undermining (7)
16 Hustles about for those seeking clues (7)
17 An occupation that republicans can regard with favour? (7)
19 Get weary with colour about when no longer working (7)
21 A body of 16 one would hardly call sweet (4)
22 Is it my surrounding that describes conditions of poor visibility? (5)
23 Exists in dual form as a goddess (4)
26 'PT, gin, nice cigars' (anag.) (are they all good for the voice?) (7,8)
27 Descriptive of a lot of the old crocks (7)
28 Brought into force by force (7)

DOWN

1 As landing places for fliers they may be fatal (7)
2 His working journey done, he travels on towards the end on reduced fare (3,3,9)
3 To be in it is all very well (4)
4 They are often purely decorative, but may be used to secure locks (7)
5 Those it supports have risen from their beds (7)
6 What many an erstwhile motorist now finds beneath him? (4)
7 Essential qualities that assist identification (15)
8 An unpleasant creature is given a short month on the work (7)
13 One could never say he lived the right way (5)
14 A mole above ground and running out to sea (5)
17 An alloy that is especially made for links (7)
18 Proceeding to mix two-thirds of an egg and an onion (5,2)
19 When a sailor gets up on a cart there may be a catch in it (3-4)
20 The only way to go to the 13 (7)

Sir Anthony Eden resigns as Prime Minister

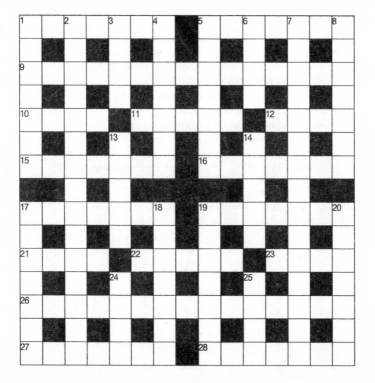

24 Angle (4)
25 Part of a credit sale (4)

14 July 1958

ACROSS

1 He sees people pop in, pop, and pop off! (10)
9 Appropriate addition to a jug of wine and a loaf of bread (4)
10 A dud not now in very poor circumstances (4,3,3)
11 Some were put to it by water, or wood (6)
12 Such a thing as a lift is a hitch to him (5)
15 You might meet him if you stray all around in the woods (5)
18 It often manifests itself as a strain (5)
19 You might certainly come to chide an arrangement of it, but not for being spineless! (7)
20 Part of a house there has been many a full house to see (5)
21 If you have hesitated, then you've had it! (5)
22 This country beheaded was a peninsula (7)
23 The little blighter that got his finally (5)
24 A month or more official for a year (5)
26 Cats and dogs come back hungry in this part of a house (5)
29 One on the rocks: just a hard case making a flabby start (6)
31 They shape well, but finish in real mix-ups (10)
32 No doubt they put somebody's nose out of joint! (4)
33 In recent wars they have been dropped (10)

DOWN

2 One of those trivial things one sees to in the morning (4)
3 Excel without a slippery customer (6)
4 Where to go if one wants to take stock? (5)
5 One may give a ring but this will do instead (5)
6 It offers an alternative to the nonsense that is going round (5)
7 Where nagging wives drive their husbands to the grave? (10)
8 Often a help to those in search of copy (10)
13 Clothed suitably to maintain one's occupation (7)
14 Red nose gives sign on reverse (7)
15 Being significantly busy on lines of communication? (10)
16 The ranting orator whose wooden expression strikes a hollow note? (3-7)
17 One does it sometimes in catching it beheaded (5)
18 She's a girl among thousands (5)
25 A go-slow notice in 18 *across* (6)
26 It upsets things for actors, but can hold things together (5)
27 The film star's favourite boy friend? (5)

114

King Faisal of Iraq assassinated

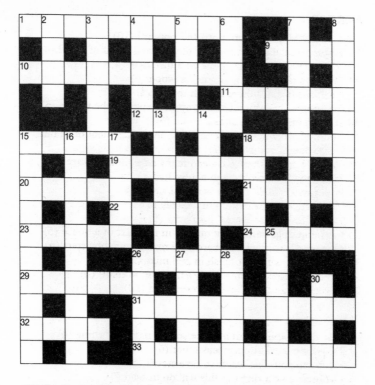

28 Gardeners who do it haphazardly don't have it curtailed (5)
30 Take a little look both ways (4)

9 October 1959

ACROSS

1 In the dawn, the dawn of love, perhaps (2,5,5)
9 Not perceived as sound (7)
10 To keep finding fault in harmony is no light matter (7)
11 What a change from icy cold weather! (4)
12 Multi-headed, flighty-bodied, imaginative author! (5)
13 It gets you down when your opponent is too good for you (4)
16 A military treatise to take back (7)
17 Ancient levy wise about an economy measure (7)
18 The oppressive influence in us shutting in the youngster (7)
21 Oil potentiality in his home-place made a big man of him (7)
23 Note on note can emanate from it (4)
24 All inside? Then do not hurry (5)
25 Favourable condition for a number of undergraduates taking a dip? (4)
28 A popular island for meeting old friends (7)
29 Not at all promising, but common sense prevails in the end (7)
30 Pants on the line for saving the hands (8-4)

DOWN

1 Put across that muddle about war (7)
2 Return of morning, as seen on the waters (4)
3 Glowing account of Soviet sporting item? (3,4)
4 Its victims suffer, but find it hard to talk (7)
5 Very long odds with only one runner? (4)
6 A blade the soldier sometimes has under the rifle (7)
7 Don't worry, he won't catch you out! (6-7)
8 Meet fresh boat in place of one of the hands (6,3,4)
14 A two degrees over killer (5)
15 They soon have this brute off in hockey (5)
19 One always looks to the best man to do it (7)
20 Such tan can prove to be constant (7)
21 Low lags came to it, but not many old lags (7)
22 Similarity in general of a record in any setting (7)
26 Go to earth? I would if he's around! (4)
27 Place needing a tenant to become a star example (4)

'Supermac' leads Tories to victory

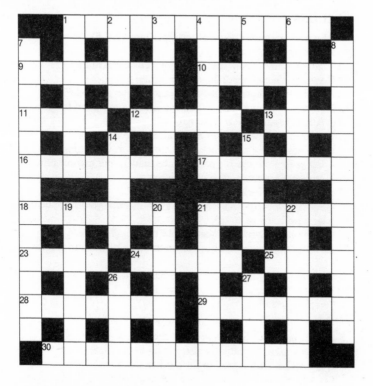

10 November 1960

ACROSS

1 Maybe a method with rhubarb that's popular in many nurseries (6,7)
10 One who makes progress only by force of arms (7)
11 Learn to shape, and fall into line (7)
12 Might this be how methodical people prefer their drink? (4)
13 A lion may feel so, surveying his family (5)
14 A leading light (4)
17 Features of the South Coast which should be eyed for their usefulness (7)
18 Pertaining to a Greek poet or perhaps a type of pigeon (7)
19 It may hold many a cup that cheers the weary Muscovite (7)
22 A training centre in Wiltshire? (7)
24 National emblem that reformed a Greek god (4)
25 One who leads us to her (5)
26 The spring of good health? (4)
29 Just one specimen, although there used to be plenty it seems (7)
30 One way to get things moving is to put them in it (7)
31 Did it take notes in the Cock Robin case? (9,4)

DOWN

2 Some motorists may be guilty of conduct meriting such a label, but not in changing gear (7)
3 Expectation that would be forlorn for a desperate enterprise (4)
4 Applies to places where people like to go (7)
5 Sadly lacking the social graces (7)
6 A stock of money concealed in a suburban kitchen (4)
7 He's cock of the walk, without a doubt (7)
8 A capital way for the ambitious politician! (7,6)
9 Such material is not necessarily from the New World (8,5)
15 Husband about fifty is by no means the master! (5)
16 There's scope for an early piece (5)
20 I'm going up to make a bet; that's an error (7)
21 Regard the spectre disintegrate (7)
22 Some of the boxers change but little, so suffer discomfort from the heat (7)
23 A supporter of old crocks? (7)

Lady Chatterley's Lover sold out

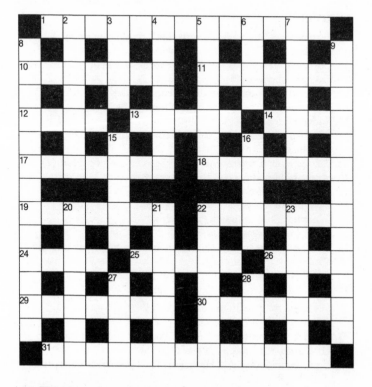

27 This ring partner is of course a ring partner (4)
28 Balm for the writer (4)

12 April 1961

ACROSS

1 Terrific suggestion that the NCB is not paying its way (8)
5 Exclude the rest of the spear-head? (6)
9 Composer has a part returned, though he has never been brought a portion (8)
10 Garments one may need on board? (6)
12 The conductor to choose what the passengers did (9)
13 Refuse a stew-hash (5)
14 What the motorist should not do in mountainous country (4)
16 Gave a fellow the wrong date (7)
19 Charge a team and get involved (7)
21 Presumably it would be made from pine (4)
24 Blooming deserter he! (5)
25 The lad has a weapon about to fall (9)
27 One who watches the pitcher after six! (6)
28 A loaf for the fourth Pole (8)
29 What the mariner does to his course if he steers wrongly (6)
30 Aimed to return about ten but troubled in mind obviously (8)

DOWN

1 BBC owe changes to this network (6)
2 Key to the small cupboard? (6)
3 Writer found in the street exhausted (5)
4 'Of temper —— as the first of May' (Tennyson) (7)
6 What the penniless profligate hopes his father will make for his improvidence (9)
7 Reverses wager on a number of games (8)
8 Comes down a point in December and reaches a conclusion (8)
11 Tiny number the root of which is often difficult to extract (4)
15 Wonder if a lot of criss-cross paths met around the pole (9)
17 Only a semi-trained tradesman, but he produces a better job (8)
18 Obviously not tied up, yet not moving in the main (8)
20 Rest of the soldiers may stand at it (4)
21 It is worth lots of money yet may be got for a song (7)
22 A summary that one should first chew over? (6)
23 At a meeting it may cause a lot of time and trouble (6)
26 A political clean-up? (5)

Yuri Gagarin becomes first man in space

5 August 1962

ACROSS

7 Stage highway robbery as in a film . . . (3,3,4-5)

8 . . . of the cowboy type (7)

10 His hiding-place is the whodunnit (7)

11 He may not be the yielding type, even though he gives (5)

12 Many an odd structure has been labelled somebody's this (5)

14 Actions to halt advances (5)

15 A mark of servitude across the shoulders (4)

16 It is drawn some way back (4)

17 Should it rain cats and dogs there should be many a one available! (4)

19 Look cheerful, and be early (4)

21 One would use it to deck 26 (5)

22 Dying in a depressingly dull sort of way . . . (5)

23 . . . but this betrayer's end took a sorrowful turn (5)

25 It can do the hit-and-run act in fleet fashion (7)

26 Somehow 21 in, at a stretch (7)

27 Lag made good, with no more time to come! (8,7)

DOWN

1 One party wrote of giving such authorisation (5,2,8)

2 Allowed up to remain outside in a dignified manner (7)

3 An air-line on the way to showing that close shaves are a thing of the past? (5)

4 The sort of meal one does not eat as it is (5)

5 In the army it does not owe its existence to promotion (7)

6 It's for rough notes, and doodling too, if you wish (10-5)

9 Should it turn up at present, someone may feel hurt (4)

10 A useful line in wood? (4)

13 Personal numerical extension of 15 (5)

14 Those who order it as a matter of course get a raw deal (5)

17 Stone causes dreadful upset in vessel (7)

18 To change one's spots at leisure? (4)

19 It might fit the Serpentine to a T! (4)

20 A word of one letter (7)

23 When this bar is busy it's open house! (5)

24 One upset in an old line foreign to us (5)

Marilyn Monroe found dead

17 April 1963

ACROSS

1 The girl's parent often appears worn out (6-2-5)
10 In the main, there's more to this than meets the eye (7)
11 A boy without a quarter gets a first-class return in the USA (7)
12 The lady's love is one distinguished by bravery (4)
13 A 14 to know in Scotland (5)
14 A symbol is reversed halfway (4)
17 A prepared statement put by the driver? (4-3)
18 With which Poseidon kept the toast at arms' length? (7)
19 Advice to one applying overmuch is no good (7)
22 It will of course stretch, and endure in an ice-break (7)
24 Smooth uniform (4)
25 It's a tell-tale type of ball bowled in cricket (5)
26 It is worn in the USA right enough, though unexpectedly (4)
29 Something fruity, ending in a fuss (7)
30 A common plant for tile breaking (7)
31 You might have got a couple of coppers for this old machine surely! (5-8)

DOWN

2 Not under-scored in cricket to exceed the limit (7)
3 They help the gardeners make a shoe-repair (4)
4 It grows wild, and must grow wild when held by a returning sailor (7)
5 An invention suitable to take in American detectives (7)
6 A flower perhaps, that may be seen in Piccadilly (4)
7 Might this music be suitable for a varsity revel? (7)
8 But his responsibility to vessels weighs heavy indeed (13)
9 Not the sort of area to attract a farmer, though (8,5)
15 Even in the hottest situations it can be game all right (5)
16 The originator of the golden handshake perhaps (5)
20 A painful thing both to have and to behold, no doubt (7)
21 Any firm referee can do this demonstration at departure (4-3)
22 One-time player strictly claiming his rights (7)
23 A new toga is pulled to pieces to make another garment (3-4)
27 Graduate gets naval support on the farm (4)
28 Some ships are constructed to hold a network (4)

Russian pianist Ashkenazy flees to Britain

12 June 1964

ACROSS

1 One of those rigid speed regulations which makes no allowances for . . . (4,3,4,4)

9 . . . square pegs? (7)

10 Its toxic effect is periodically demonstrated in fact and fiction (7)

11 A place one old soldier found ideal for escapism (4)

12 Express the definition of a pilot? (5)

13 At first Ludwig returned the scurvy treatment (4)

16 Deceitful to imprison the bird so harshly (7)

17 It's often all that's left to other people (7)

18 There might be a seamy side to the story of their fall in the field (7)

21 This Indian scorns Western clothes, but has warm cover (7)

23 'And I said to the man who stood at the gate of the —— ' (Haskins) (4)

24 Miss Hill, read by gaslight? (5)

25 Flinched, but hasn't run away (4)

28 All drew round and agreed (7)

29 A mere particle of electricity by one account, but actually a fantastic amount! (7)

30 A personal line controlled by fateful sister (3,6,2,4)

DOWN

1 Resolutely persists in solving the problem of driving home one's point? (7,4,2,2)

2 Ludicrous, distorted and rib-splitting lies (7)

3 Only six in age, and so greedy! (4)

4 Show little Diana's show (7)

5 He does what he does gamely often, but just for fun, they say (7)

6 Shot into the rubbish (4)

7 Lacking the dignity of a title? (7)

8 A first-class opportunity in the race for promotion, maybe (9,6)

14 Came to some conclusion (5)

15 Even Philistines say it holds literary possibilities (5)

19 Precursor, namely, of Chaplin, and Drake, and other amusing men (7)

Nelson Mandela jailed for life

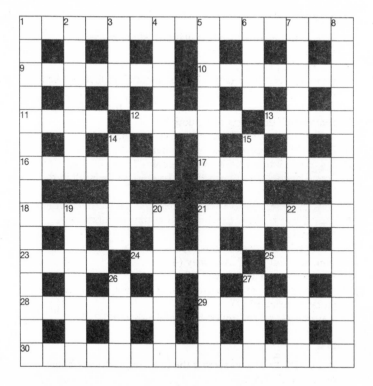

20 Swathe divine authority in 'Wild Wales'? (7)
21 A resting-place purely for old fossils (4-3)
22 Most of the craft which made a famous crossing of the Pacific (3-4)
26 The inspiration behind many an over-optimistic thought (4)
27 Players can learn from it what to expect of the pitch (4)

1965–74

Much is written of the Swinging Sixties and Seventies; but on reflection this era contains merely the aftershocks of the seismic upheavals of the previous decade.

In 1965 the USA became more deeply involved in the Vietnam War, Churchill died and the death penalty was abolished in Britain. The following year Mrs Gandhi became prime minister of India and South Africa's Prime Minister Verwoerd was assassinated – but on the first of February that year there was still space on the *Telegraph*'s front page to bemoan the fact that England were 123 for five against Australia in the fourth Test in Adelaide. The morning had started well 'with no greater shock to English nerves than a forward stroke by Cowdrey off Chappell's second ball which flew uppishly through the vacant gully'. (Even if you don't have the faintest idea what they are talking about, you know it has to be an Englishman's voice.) But disaster struck 20 minutes before lunch when both Cowdrey and Smith lost their wickets. It didn't get better – England lost by an innings and nine runs.

The world heard that Dr Christiaan Barnard had performed the first heart transplant operation in December 1967, but earlier that year, in the summer, *The Daily Telegraph* crossword had also suffered a transplant – to television. It was the first – and, in my opinion, the *only* successful – appearance of the *Telegraph*'s cryptic crosswords on the box. The BBC2 programme *Crossword on Two* had an initial run of 13 weeks. *The Daily Telegraph* contributed puzzles for seven of the programmes, and *The Times* took care of the other six. The *Telegraph*'s contribution came from the paper's regular compilers, Barnard and Cash, edited by Margaret Binstead. Opposing teams of three-a-side competed to solve the puzzles within the allotted half an hour. The experiment proved so popular that the series was extended for a further 26 programmes. An extra problem for the programme makers, the compilers and Miss Binstead was to find the right standard of puzzle which would take six brains 30 minutes to solve!

The late sixties saw the assassination of Martin Luther King, the election of President Nixon in the USA, the ill-fated Prague Spring reforms in Czechoslovakia, student riots in Paris and the resignation of President De Gaulle; Golda Meir became Israel's prime minister and a man walked on the moon. In September 1968, *The Daily Telegraph* gave front-page prominence to the Federal Nigerian government's agreement to allow the Red Cross to fly relief supplies into Biafra. The region's unsuccessful secession from Nigeria was possibly the first post-independence war in Africa, but certainly not the last nor the only one to use famine as a weapon.

The seventies blew in with the election of President Allende in Chile and the lowering of Britain's age of majority to 18. Huge demonstrations against the Vietnam War took place in Washington, Idi Amin came to power in Uganda, the UK adopted decimal currency and two years later in 1973 joined the European Economic Union.

Changes were also afoot in *The Daily Telegraph*'s crossword department: two new occasional compilers were brought in to supplement the existing two-man team. Leslie Stokes started creating crosswords to entertain his fellow officers during the Second World War, when he was assistant purser on board the troopship *Highland Monarch*. The prize was a bottle of whisky. After the war he took up setting crosswords as a full-time career. Tom Pritchard took up crossword compiling in retirement. A gentle man with a consuming love of music, he and his wife lived in a tidy house in Lytham St Annes. Both Stokes and Pritchard contributed one puzzle per fortnight. This eased the load on Cash and Barnard and allowed a little more variety into the *Telegraph* crossword.

By this time, the crossword was firmly established as a necessity to a vast number of *Telegraph* readers. A marketing survey from the late 1960s shows that around 15 per cent of the readership gave the crossword as their main reason for taking the paper and a further 15 per cent said the crossword was the second/third reason for reading the paper. With a readership of approximately three million that means around one million people were tackling the crossword. A daunting prospect for any crossword compiler.

Let me end the preface to this decade with two nicely contrasting little stories both found next to the crossword on the back page of *The Daily Telegraph* on Monday, 19 February 1973.

The first was:

FOUR MURDERED IN MOUNTAINS
By our New York Staff

The bodies of four long-haired youths were found in a mountain shack at Santa Cruz, California, during the weekend. It brought the total of murders committed in the area to 13 in six weeks. Only one of the bodies of the latest victims has been identified . . .

The second story just five or six centimetres below was:

FIRE KILLS CALVES

Eighteen Friesian heifer calves were burned to death yesterday when fire damaged a barn at Mr Clifford Holt's Droke Farm, East Dean, near Chichester, Sussex. The alarm was raised by Christopher Fry, the poet and dramatist, who lives in a cottage nearby.

The Daily Telegraph

and Morning Post

No. 34606. LONDON, SATURDAY, DECEMBER 4, 1965.   Printed in LONDON and MANCHESTER. Price 4d.

ULTIMATUM BY AFRICAN STATES

Britain must crush Smith by Dec. 15

DEATH WARNS WILSON AGAINST FORCE

Organisation for African Unity divided in Addis Ababa last night that its 36-member bloc freed diplomatic relations with Britain by Dec. 15 if she has not ended Rhodesia's rebellion by then.

...

RISING ASSETS

...

BLOCKADE THREATENED

By IAN COLVIN
Daily Telegraph Staff Correspondent
ADDIS ABABA, Friday.

...

Salisbury Bank chiefs suspended

...

PEOPLE'S INTERESTS
Order's main purpose.

...

QUEEN REJECTS SMITH'S ADVICE ON GOVERNOR

Daily Telegraph Commonwealth Affairs Correspondent

...

FRENCH FUTURE AT STAKE

Daily Telegraph Staff Correspondent

...

PREMIUM BOND DRAW

...

Index to Other Pages

A picture by flash of R.A.F. Javelins of fighters and transport aircraft lined up in Ndola airport before taking off for Zambia yesterday.
Below: Mr. Beniedux, Commonwealth Secretary, walking past one of the fighters where he inspected them at Ndola.
(Report and map—P11)

7 pc MORTGAGES LIKELY IN NEW YEAR

SOCIETIES' RIFT ON RATES

DAILY TELEGRAPH CITY STAFF

...

Pirates not to get radio licences

...

3 KLANSMEN GAOLED FOR 10 YEARS

Daily Telegraph Staff Correspondent
NEW YORK, Friday.

...

EX-B.P.C CHIEF RETURNING 'THIS MONTH'

Daily Telegraph Correspondent
SALISBURY.

...

RUSSIA ATTEMPTS MOON LANDING

...

LATE NEWS

CRICKET

...

VIET CONG BLOW UP U.S. ARMY BILLET

DAWN ATTACK IN SAIGON

SAIGON, Saturday.

VIET CONG raiders blasted an American Army billet in Saigon with bombs and explosives today. Hospitals said so many dead and wounded were brought in that it was impossible to count them.

...

ARMED MAN THREATENES POLICE

...

Lawful charges

...

Reinforcements sent

...

PICASSO OPERATION

...

Personal Column—Page 1

6 September 1965

ACROSS

1 A fur that is usually dark brown or black, and . . . (5)
4 . . . another of exactly the same kind (9)
8 A Greek goddess was barely surprised by him! (7)
9 A negro I displaced when flints had gone out of use (4,3)
10 Type of jug we return with little hesitation (4)
11 A creature caught with a rod? Yes, a rod! (5)
12 Felt strangely abandoned (4)
15 Polishing agent responsible for Mr Wilson's endurance in office? (9,4)
17 Something written just for money (7,6)
20 Nothing to be particularly fond of! (4)
21 No doubly soft lining is essential for the baby! (5)
22 Filled with eager desire, the great singer makes a comeback (4)
25 They supply tea with or without sugar! (7)
26 Part of the USSR where men break into song, apparently (7)
27 Its importance in volume is purely nominal (5-4)
28 A subject on which there may well be variations (5)

DOWN

1 Its unfortunate members are likely to derive most benefit from it! (5,4)
2 Form of attack for which some artillerymen are required (7)
3 Flat into which two will go? (4)
4 They are not things certain railwaymen should go by (6,7)
5 A sacred figure I commit to memory (4)
6 He plays for 20 *across* (7)
7 One must make some effort to do this oneself (5)
9 Evidently not a tree growing straight up a ramp! (8,5)
13 A rush-basket needing the most careful handling (5)
14 A mole of an intensely black colour? (5)
16 Poor rider that has somehow come unstuck! (5-4)
18 Announce what supplies will do if not replenished (4,3)
19 '—— is a kind of wild justice' (Bacon) (7)
20 A clue not difficult to pick up? (5)
23 The river from which one never returns (4)
24 It follows me back to 18, maybe (4)

India attacks Pakistan

4 March 1966

1 South of France spot that somehow caught 'er napping (9)
9 He made one of the Italians (6)
10 1st of December: got married; cut down drastically! (9)
11 Sounds the chap to go round on one wheel (6)
12 No sea monster, Hobbes's (9)
13 On one's mark to show a whole lot of teeth? (3,3)
17 An adverb, still it may be a conjunction too (3)
19 A darlin' colleen (7)
20 Thus enfeebled, grandfather gets the wind up, no doubt! (3,4)
21 Thirty-one days of doubtful significance (3)
23 Carry on again with the summary (6)
27 Group of Sinaitic rules that Moses broke (9)
28 One swallow does not make it much less (6)
29 Ship's officer needs freshening up; no one can go on board! (9)
30 This bell rings a dire message in maritime affairs (6)
31 Burning sound of roast pork (9)

DOWN

2 Time, but not enough for light refreshment (6)
3 He is providing a little incentive, one hears (6)
4 Light blue Isis? (6)
5 Outstanding music-hall comedian, but vinegary (7)
6 He took not the wilder road to Samarkand (9)
7 Strikers' meeting at which a stoppage is usually called for (9)
8 Silver in a state across the Atlantic (9)
14 It is about little people and for them (5-4)
15 They're going round the town making a revolutionary fashion call (9)
16 Mona has it altered for her (9)
17 Vegetable that will be back in 21 (3)
18 It has often led to conversion on the field of battle! (3)
22 A more worthy friend to the criminal (7)
24 Doubly Caesar's, this war (6)
25 'The justice . . . With eyes severe and beard of —— cut' (*As You Like It*) (6)
26 He's only now arrived (6)

Lennon says Beatles more popular than Jesus

10 May 1967

ACROSS

8 It's intended to lure one in a sports club, perhaps (4)
9 Little silver article for an Eastern commander (3)
10 Smooth coat to go over me in a backward country road (6)
11 " ' —— ' bright, Like golden lamps in a green night" (Marvell: *Bermudas*) (6)
12 I can turn and I frenziedly eat to get going maybe! (8)
13 Where trains may be expected to run normally? (2,3,5,5)
15 Law they amend with ample resources (7)
17 Worshipping a circle about to perform (7)
20 A firm believer in self-rule, he completely disregards convention (1,3,4,7)
23 A brawler honoured as an expert on figures . . . (8)
25 . . . and one who shouldn't be seen in public! (6)
26 Not a single answer? (6)
27 A city in which we feel younger (3)
28 Kind of lighting the Tyne-Tees area has on (4)

DOWN

1 Empty grain store broken by engineers (6)
2 Good man to handle wrong nom de plume for a French novelist (8)
3 China needs it, diplomatically and otherwise! (7,8)
4 Decayed promises to pay for hired transport? (7)
5 Highly-seasoned grill that cook played Old Harry with! (8,7)
6 It backs a successful play inside a faraway island (6)
7 A fabric known by the touch? (4)
14 One out for a long time (3)
16 The Spanish pound, once used as a measure (3)
18 I'd resent going out or staying in! (8)
19 He runs a newspaper, possibly (7)
21 In Norfolk a current novel backed with a quantity of money (6)
22 Some instruction 25 could scarcely have! (6)
24 Too heavy a bird to become airborne, naturally (4)

Rolling Stones on drugs charges

20 August 1968

ACROSS

1 Downtrodden workers scattered all over a bus (5,6)
8 Early retirement should help one to recover from it (4,2,5)
11 A king I'd deprived of water (4)
12 Double act once seen in Mauritius (4)
13 Buttons always poetic within the nobility (7)
15 At first one is taken in by very French dresses (7)
16 The best watchmen? (5)
17 They provide hospitality in more ways than one (4)
18 Evidently a stop that won't work? (2,2)
19 A jolly little newspaper chief prepared to defend himself! (5)
21 Snacks from street vendors do when a troubled ghost is around! (3,4)
22 'Sport that wrinkled Care —— ' (Milton: *L'Allegro*) (7)
23 The state that has vanished in North-East Italy (4)
26 Some types of foreign currency (4)
27 The shining light of the ironing board? (7,4)
28 Thwarted lovers have often been known to make a dash for it (6,5)

DOWN

2 Old arrangement about a consignment of goods, maybe (4)
3 They came to plunder a Cambridge college after six (7)
4 Remained to be relatively progressive (4)
5 Quarters no good in wagers (7)
6 Put to some purpose in famous edifices (4)
7 He brightened up the late Victorian scene (11)
8 The exile isn't allowed to occupy a palatial residence, for instance (4,2,5)
9 A man with a private income? He won't put up much of a struggle! (4,7)
10 It continually provides entertainment (3-4,4)
14 Vessels we hedge about with hesitant remarks (5)
15 Requested a new desk (5)
19 Averse to profit in a small way (7)
20 Another raider's corresponding start (4,3)
24 Constantly put right after the previous day (4)
25 Peruvian prince in a hundred turns (4)
26 A step one quietly goes over (4)

Soviet tanks invade Czechoslovakia

21 July 1969

ACROSS

1 Accidental accommodation for two families under one roof (6,4)
6 Pronounce corporal punishment, though maybe he deserved capital punishment (4)
9 150 on the next page, but fly over (6-4)
10 Enter into contest with the West. That is one aspect (4)
13 Worthless French currency broken by recurrent anger is not trifling (7)
15 Horse tender from the stable (6)
16 French gentleman, not the same one, but a parent nonetheless (6)
17 Like any unprofitable investment with no attraction (7,8)
18 Want a knight taken in by a Cheshire banker (6)
20 Old army officer flown by the navy (6)
21 Mean Ebenezer? (7)
22 It resembles somewhat a twisting vine (4)
25 If I tail car carelessly that will be unnatural (10)
26 An instruction to line up the pages (4)
27 Be in false teeth for capital investments! (10)

DOWN

1 Five hundred and one fish (4)
2 Immediately after incorporating the Post Office in the United Nations (4)
3 Airs suggesting falsehoods uttered with some hesitation (6)
4 Conforming is fine, limiting everyone in spirit and a lot the other way (7,4,4)
5 Warning given by a wall-painting hung the wrong way (6)
7 The third R in curriculum (10)
8 It may be novel; at least it should be novel in style (3,7)
11 Knocked down, having made six deliveries (6,4)
12 No change in the gilt-edged market. Absolutely steady (5-5)
13 New variety of roses in maturity, it would seem (7)
14 Not all, but a single entity as yet unidentified (7)
19 Create new card game (6)
20 One given to self-expression (6)
23 Gunners leave rapier on the sea-front (4)
24 A cross in 7 (4)

The first man walks on the moon

14 April 1970

ACROSS

1 Which of our native birds has to be heavily subsidised? (7,4)

8 Largely where one might expect to see a star (2,5,4)

11 Has grown strangely partial (4)

12 It may indicate boredom, taking the northern route back (4)

13 Misplaced ceremony includes a bun for the platform (7)

15 Take a late meal with Army technicians of the highest standing (7)

16 Drops from exhaustion? (5)

17 A state that requires relief, and . . . (4)

18 . . . one in it abandoned (4)

19 & 21 What motoring schools do for key men on 1? (5,7)

22 'In some melodious plot of —— green' (Keats: *Ode to a Nightingale*) (7)

23 A chore with no alternative but pain (4)

26 Very seldom caught in the first hour of the day? (4)

27 The board conceals a motive of disloyal character (11)

28 Childishly? Only to a limited extent (2,1,5,3)

DOWN

2 Courses put on by successful partnerships (4)

3 A sweet and short answer for those who follow Highland fashions (7)

4 Dramatic name for a small wood (4)

5 Forcibly removes one in an odd stupor (4,3)

6 Small railway quartet going over the scene of one of Henry IV's triumphs (4)

7 Wild tiger Danton found on the coast of Sussex (11)

8 Eupeptic attacker of sport? (6,5)

9 It impressively records impulsive messages from distant places (4-7)

10 A handy pointer (5,6)

14 King surrounded by timid females and water-carriers (5)

15 Indian gentleman who plays a Hibernian part (5)

19 They work hard and turn kind about the beginning of the year (7)

20 The trawlermen's dance that appeals to sporting girls? (7)

24 Engineers brought up in a land of poesy (4)

Explosion cripples Apollo 13

25 She rings when the artist is out (4)
26 A £2 duck turned over to culinary use in Spain (4)

24 April 1971

ACROSS

6 A stay-at-home who keeps looking for amusement? (10,3)

8 A paper freshly come out (6)

9 Pupil power? (8)

10 Weighty piece of 2 (3)

11 A fine yarn men love about Richard I! (6)

12 Gets stiff with cold, maybe (8)

14 Badly damaged old English settler taken in by a doctor (7)

16 She pretends recasts upset her (7)

20 A remote island terrier of mine? (8)

23 Lowly fellow turning in when there's food around (6)

24 Midas topped and tailed her! (3)

25 Not avowedly exposing the misdeeds of others (8)

26 We are held back by a common informer on the Trent (6)

27 Ultimately correct position for a gangway seat (5,2,3,3)

DOWN

1 Not keeping the same integral formation (8)

2 A harmonic richness of suggestion? (8)

3 Basic element that makes odd sense to the civil engineer (7)

4 Style supported by the Navy of today (6)

5 A place designed for desk work, not skating? (6)

6 Recommended first of course! (6,1,6)

7 A free fight with all the hatches open? (2,5,6)

13 Obtained some sago to eat (3)

15 The meadow under which the state school is (3)

17 Red Indian coachmen's organisation (8)

18 'Peace hath her victories no less —— than war' (Milton: *To the Lord General Cromwell*) (8)

19 They are entitled to pass over other men on the board (7)

21 A reform needed by shopkeepers (6)

22 They can't help acting irrationally (6)

500,000 in US anti-Vietnam War demo

25 February 1972

ACROSS

1 In no condition to act, so came to a fresh arrangement (8)
5 It ran around mortified (6)
9 Individual copies returned with speed (8)
10 Pleased about being brought in, though looked far from it! (6)
11 Neatly conclude a postponed club game? (5,3)
12 Dormant fish turned into a snake (6)
14 Not the first ex-Prime Minister to define a weekend cottage! (6,4)
18 Debating point that cannot be conducive to harmony (10)
22 In their moment of triumph they sank beneath the waves (1-5)
23 Heather following another girl in Cabinet office (8)
24 Small band of Marines in strange tale (6)
25 It may strengthen or weaken an army . . . (8)
26 . . . to engage in its service (6)
27 A spot of comfort for the local visitor (8)

DOWN

1 One who has benefited from America's troubles (6)
2 Maybe one needs to get this to plan the proceedings in detail (3,3)
3 Traffic-bound unit producing a string of invective! (6)
4 Essential equipment for the consumer? (3,2,5)
6 A friend with odd ideas for stakes (8)
7 Attacked and made to run? (6,2)
8 A diver or bather interrupted by an American lawyer (8)
13 Natural hue that makes one pass over the ceremonial speech (10)
15 Precise bill supported by a junior minister (8)
16 Unpretentious bench with half a bent nail at each end (8)
17 They don't believe he requires capital in Greece (8)
19 Having nothing particular to do, I'd fish (6)
20 In a penalty it is of limited significance (6)
21 A representative business (6)

Miners call off seven-week coal strike

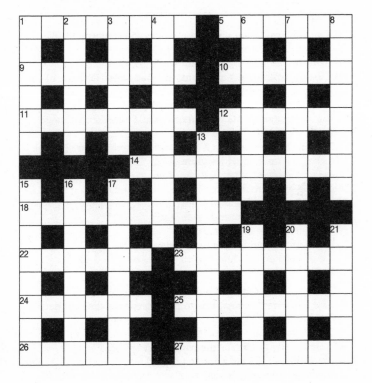

8 April 1973

ACROSS

1 The die-hards basically employed in road construction? (4,4)
5 Appropriate line between a small pair (6)
9 Flattery that won't wash? But it will! (4,4)
10 Threads from which briefs may be made (6)
11 Oriental lawyers who sadly recall the past (8)
13 Its meaning is hidden in a 21, possibly (6)
14 Warily reluctant to make a start (3)
16 A middle course for the consumer (6)
19 I return to make a call about violence in the streets (7)
20 A compact old linear measure (6)
21 Its price goes up when it's cut (3)
26 A cape in South America (6)
27 Not a working institution (4-4)
28 A case for capital equipment (3-3)
29 It braves a new order, yet trembles (8)
30 Abandon the struggle against the enemy (6)
31 What mice try to avoid when crossing roads? (4-4)

DOWN

1 She had written about what the meat was, to save money (6)
2 Plundered by the soldiery, the king and I ran away (6)
3 Isaac's new drug (6)
4 Responds to stimulus and gives an encore? (6)
6 Providing a ruling about two gin cocktails (8)
7 Porridge-making is hardly what one expects of this area of France! (8)
8 Given another form (8)
12 Do a great deal of damage by using different threats (7)
15 Mixed type of food (3)
16 Object of life or death? (3)
17 Stumbles over the coal-scuttle. How careless! (8)
18 Business tycoons writing about a perplexed agent (8)
19 The morning or afternoon jam session? (4,4)
22 Islamic city I named incorrectly (6)
23 Manifestations of a violent nature (6)
24 ' —— thy habit as thy purse can buy' (*Hamlet*, Act I) (6)
25 A check on those who live in the country (6)

Picasso dies

8 August 1974

ACROSS

1 Boiled sweet with a fruity flavour (4-4)
5 Good man with wrong name for a floral feature (6)
9 A final observation? (4,4)
10 They generally indicate the way things are going (6)
11 After all, I manage without epic inspiration (8)
12 I'm held back by a bunch of crooks operating at the Casino (6)
14 Galician town sourly embroiled with force (10)
18 Bloodsuckers showing Jewish religious leader round a South American capital (10)
22 He achieved fictitious fame in jungle fighting (6)
23 Old French statute that dealt exclusively with women of high birth (5,3)
24 He takes odd bets about Pindar's birthplace (6)
25 A letter that sounds soft (8)
26 Regularly move in a whirl of activity? (6)
27 A drink of tea I sent out (8)

DOWN

1 Course of action recommended to one who lacks assurance (6)
2 Not disposed of for cash (6)
3 Sweet name for a girl (6)
4 Twelve-inch photos giving evidence of steps taken (10)
6 Arrogant blend of vinegar (8)
7 Creature that may pray as climbing the right side of a log (8)
8 Features about merry little bunches (8)
13 Share, after a fashion, not recommended by extremists (10)
15 I take Timothy up over a rocky height – he follows (8)
16 Ensure it will make you rapacious (8)
17 Evidently not a main factor in business (8)
19 Blooming layabouts Christians are asked to consider! (6)
20 Far from obdurate one set outside (6)
21 Sort of hats we put binding round (6)

Nixon resigns over Watergate affair

1975–84

On 30 April 1975 the war in Vietnam ended as the government in Saigon announced its unconditional surrender to the Vietcong. American and other foreigners scrambled to board US helicopters for evacuation from Saigon, only hours before North Vietnamese troops arrived to seize control of the city. Many South Vietnamese officials struggled to find a place on the boats and helicopters as well. The image of that desperate scramble to get out of Saigon was to stick in the mind of anyone who saw it on television or read of it in the newspaper.

So how comforting it was three months later to read of the 50th anniversary of *The Daily Telegraph* crossword. To mark the occasion, a special book was published featuring a crossword from each year of its existence and in that week each of the three winners of the Saturday Prize Crossword competition received a case of champagne in addition to the usual prize of £7 worth of book tokens.

In the following year Concorde took its first flight; Jimmy Carter (a Democrat) was elected president of the

United States; the architect of the People's Republic of China, Mao Tse-tung, died; James Callaghan became prime minister and the Peace March by Irishwomen took place; and in June, the *Telegraph* reported the discovery of a *Daily Telegraph* crossword club in Geneva:

> It seems that 30 English-speaking residents there have banded together to solve the crossword on a competitive basis. Each day they hand in the puzzle completed as far as they can manage.
>
> For each unsolved clue they pay 10 centimes (about two pence) and a failure to attempt the puzzle at all incurs a fine of two francs (45p). At the end of the month they take the money and treat themselves to dinner.
>
> The convenor of the club, a professional interpreter . . . confesses to doing the crossword while pretending to make notes at dull official engagements.

In 1977 – the year of the Queen's Silver Jubilee – a major event took place on the *Telegraph*'s crossword scene – Margaret Binstead retired after some 20 years as crossword editor. May Abbott, an accomplished compiler and feature writer, took over for a month or so – she had written an authoritative introduction to *The Daily Telegraph 50th Anniversary Crossword Book* and was familiar with Miss Binstead's methods – followed by Keith Jenkins (now editor of the international *Weekly Telegraph*) for six weeks, before I took over as the permanent new crossword editor.

Keith Jenkins and Martin Sarson – both sub-editors on *The Daily Telegraph* at that time – had for many years acted as a second pair of eyes for Margaret Binstead. The process by which the crossword leaps from the compiler's mind to the pages of the paper is by no means a simple one. The compiler creates the crossword and sends it to the editor who has it typeset. It is then sent to a sub-editor (Keith Jenkins, Martin Sarson, A. N. Other, etc.) who solves the puzzle, and makes comments and suggests alterations. Meanwhile, it is also being solved by the editor herself (I don't think there has ever been a 'himself' on this paper), who makes her own comments and suggestions. The crossword editor may then marry together some or all of her own and her subs' suggestions and alter the original crossword accordingly. It is then printed in the paper, together with the previous day's crossword puzzle solution (or on Mondays, a prize crossword solution).

April Fool's Day fell on a Saturday in 1978 so the Saturday prize crossword was a little different from usual. The clues were very easy as cryptic clues go but the solutions – apart from 1 across *Backwardly* – had to be entered in reverse order for the solution grid to hang together properly. An intelligence test for our solvers, who rose to the occasion magnificently.

The birth of the world's first test-tube baby was announced in Manchester that July. Louise Brown was born shortly before midnight in the Oldham and District General Hospital. Weighing 5lb 12oz (2.61 kg), the baby was delivered by caesarean section because her mother, Lesley Brown, was suffering from toxaemia.

Four months earlier, a New York housewife had won what was billed as the first annual American crossword puzzle tournament. Nancy Schuster had swiftly deduced that 'Post-Watergate depression' (4,4) was *Mopy Dick*, a deduction that would leave most modern British cruciverbalists a trifle perplexed, even if they did know that President Richard Nixon's administration had been brought down by a huge political scandal, dubbed Watergate, during the early 1970s. The tournament's title was hardly accurate since a number of crossword championships were held in New York in the 1920s, when the puzzles first became widely popular among newspaper and magazine readers.

The Shah of Persia fled Iran in January 1979 and a month later Ayatollah Khomeini returned after a 14-year exile and soon became the head of the country's Islamic government. On 4 November, Iranian militants stormed the United States Embassy in Tehran and took approximately 70 Americans captive. This terrorist act triggered the most profound crisis of the Carter presidency and began a personal ordeal for Jimmy Carter and the American people that lasted 444 days. In that same year in April, on a much lighter note, *The Daily Telegraph* had this paragraph on its back page:

> Police are trying to identify a man suffering from loss of memory who is said to be adept at completing the crossword puzzle in *The Daily Telegraph*. The man, aged between 26 and 30, was found at the Reference Library, Swindon, Wiltshire.

Possibly his state of mind had been caused by trying to solve the paper's puzzle printed two days earlier – a special crossword for St George's Day (23 April). The previous year there had been special crosswords for St David's Day, St Patrick's Day and St Andrew's Day, but nothing on St George's Day as that fell on a Sunday in 1978. A deluge of letters greeted this omission, including one from the Dragon threatening to come over and engulf the crossword office in its fiery breath! Discretion being the better part of valour, a special St George's Day crossword appeared on Monday, 23 April 1979. The following month Margaret Thatcher became Britain's first woman prime minister.

Nineteen eighty passed in a blur – Rhodesia gained independence as the socialist republic of Zimbabwe with Robert Mugabe installed as its Marxist leader; the SAS stormed London's Iranian embassy freeing 19 hostages, and the Moscow Olympics opened without the United States, West Germany or Japan, who boycotted the event in protest at the Soviet invasion of Afghanistan the previous December. And in a small paragraph on the back page of the paper on that same day, 19 July, a major catastrophe was reported:

> Torrential rain followed by severe floods forced the evacuation of about a million people, Indian news agencies reported yesterday. United News of India said 325 people have died, mainly in Uttar Pradesh where the Ganges has overflowed.

In 1981 Roy Jenkins, Shirley Williams, David Owen and Bill Rodgers founded the short-lived Social Democratic Party, Prince Charles married Lady Diana Spencer and the government announced that the 'recession was over'. The following year unemployment in Great Britain passed the three million mark for the first time since the 1930s and the Falkland Islands were seized by Argentina. It is worth recounting a brief conversation between myself and the then editor of *The Daily Telegraph*, William Deedes (now Lord Deedes), during the Falklands War. He was of course aware of the tale of the D-Day code words and the *Telegraph* crossword, and one day he asked me, very casually, to assure him that 'there were no unfortunate words in the crossword'. I did, naturally, assure him of this.

On a more felicitous note *The Daily Telegraph* reported that:

> An Easter swimming marathon in aid of the Mary Rose Trust at Victoria Park pool, Portsmouth, raised £34,500. Some of Britain's top athletes were among the 147 teams which entered the event.

On 10 June 1983, Mrs Thatcher won a second term in office after a landslide victory by the Conservatives, and on the same day *The Daily Telegraph* published a rather bizarre little story following the previous year's victorious conclusion to the Falklands War:

> About 30 firms have been asked to submit ideas to the Defence Department on ways to provide extra

storage capacity on the Falklands. Suggestions include sinking surplus ships to the seabed, with extra warehouses built on top of them; building a harbour in Britain which would be towed out in parts and joined together; and buying a dry-dock now in Malta. A Government decision is likely in July.

During this period of the late 1970s and early 1980s *Telegraph* crossword solvers were coming to grips with a new compiler, Bert Danher. An accomplished musician and crossword compiler, Bert was to compile almost 1,000 puzzles for *The Daily Telegraph* before his sudden death in 2002. May Abbott was also contributing crosswords on an occasional basis, so the *Telegraph* had six compilers: Abbott, Barnard, Cash, Danher, Pritchard and Stokes.

The period ended with the year 1984 which, although not as grim as George Orwell's novel led us to believe, was a far from happy one. Andropov, leader of the Soviet Union, died and was succeeded by Chernenko – at 72 the oldest man ever to take over as Soviet leader; the virus which caused AIDS was identified; film star and actor Richard Burton died, and on 13 October an IRA bomb went off in the Grand Hotel, Brighton, during the Conservative Party conference. Three people were killed, and several MPs and members of their families were injured. Mrs Thatcher, the prime minister, was unharmed.

COLOUR MAGAZINE TODAY
FINAL*

The Daily Telegraph

No. 37574. LONDON, FRIDAY, MAY 16, 1975.

Printed in LONDON and MANCHESTER

7p

J.TREVOR
Property Consultants

U.S. death toll may reach 16

FORD'S GAMBLE PAYS OFF

Cambodia raises white flag and frees seized crew

THE BOLDEST gamble in President Ford's career ended in total triumph yesterday. The last of the American Marines sent in to rescue the U.S. freighter Mayaguez and her crew, captured by Khmer Rouge Communists three days ago, were airlifted from Kam Tang Island, 30 miles off the Cambodian mainland.

American Marines running ...

Khmers Rouges humbled

By BRUCE LOUDON in Bangkok

Wilson defends attitude to economy

By DAVID HARRIS Political Staff

THE Prime Minister last night defended himself from the whole armed criticism that he gave the impression of complacency over the state of the economy in his marathon television performance on Sunday.

Wilson on Nixon—P6;
Commons—P4;
Special Article—P12;
Frank Johnson—Back Page

FORCES TO GET 25 pc PAY RISE

By Air Cdre E. W. Donaldson Air Correspondent

Navy to get 25 Sea Harriers

By DESMOND WETTERN

THE Navy is to be equipped with Sea Harriers, the naval version of the vertical take-off fighter, and has spent £70m on pre-production projects, Mr Mallalieu, Minister of Defence, said yesterday.

Prestige is enhanced

By STEPHEN BARBER in Washington

PRESIDENT FORD took the narrowest to recover the Mayaguez has propelled America with the first good news in months out of Asia and enhanced his personal authority and prestige domestically in the process.

STERLING'S DECLINE HALTED

STAY-OUT VOTE AT CHRYSLERS

By Our Industrial Staff

DRY WEATHER LIKELY IN MOST AREAS

SPECIAL HUNT FOR BODY OF LORD LUCAN

High-performance electronic watch at an unbeatable price!

BULOVA
ACCUTRON

11 February 1975

ACROSS

1 Admitted nothing matched, after all (7)
5 He's a tryer when needled, hang it! (7)
9 Resting places changed by long use (7)
10 Mr Fox cutting up red yarn (7)
11 Backing order to finish or give a song (9)
12 Boy the French used for cooking (5)
13 Lamination essential to the battery (5)
15 Energetic people, currently dangerous (4,5)
17 Inherited from our forebears, Lancaster is re-planned (9)
19 Beastly coat returned to us for a ruddy English sovereign! (5)
22 500 in old Rome fit to live (5)
23 How to make money: be impudent – it adds flavour! (4,5)
25 Animal taking on Smith, the dark blue (7)
26 Unbeliever in ploughed field (7)
27 A drink for a man on board (7)
28 Made certain conclusion about complicated ruse (7)

DOWN

1 & 17 **down** Clean bill of health at the convent? That's as may be! (3,4,3,4)
2 Duly ran wild where dirty linen is washed (7)
3 In law a German outlay for the better (5)
4 A man of spirit, but he keeps still (9)
5 Shoot, derogatory young man! (5)
6 A craft, though obsolete, will perhaps flourish (9)
7 Hero worship went swimmingly for him (7)
8 Don again to adjust the balance (7)
14 Deciding about finding the answer to this? (9)
16 Saintly bearer of a loving message (9)
17 See 1 *down*
18 Cameron disturbed a fiddling township! (7)
20 One who starts to sink (7)
21 Sped round 45 inches literally analysed (7)
23 Otherwise meant the nominal 20 of Impressionism (5)
24 Riddles (5)

Thatcher elected as Conservative leader

5 April 1976

ACROSS

1 Outmoded type of railway signal (5-7)
8 The lumberjack's progress record? (3-4)
9 Meat and drink to the invalid, maybe (4,3)
11 High mass at night in a French town? (7)
12 Satellite retrospectively allowed to play a leading role (7)
13 I am in a position to make a reasoned assumption (5)
14 In its heyday it offered wonderful variety (5-4)
16 Aware of the writing material about at the moment? (2,3,4)
19 Deep split in the West (5)
21 Silly creatures holding the negative of an Italian port (7)
23 'When the wind is southerly, I know a hawk from a —— '
   (*Hamlet*, Act 2) (7)
24 Minister taken round a nuclear establishment (7)
25 Studio that is outwardly peculiarly alert (7)
26 Compact outcome of a private war? (6,6)

DOWN

1 Messages in which vulgar language is brought up (7)
2 Caustic form of tender love (7)
3 Reconciliation officer at work behind the scenes? (4-2,3)
4 A custom Jack has to strike about (5)
5 Bill presented to the Artillery for varnish? (7)
6 A title I ordered for a girl (7)
7 Quick-moving little bounder from South Africa (12)
10 Spring water (5,7)
15 Move wildly to strike against nothing (3,3,3)
17 The cargo capacity no agent can provide (7)
18 Parties appeal to him (7)
19 Army fireman with a prickly rhubarb (7)
20 Tilly, all excited, set about us with vigour (7)
22 It flies down on a thistle, perhaps (5)

Reclusive millionaire Howard Hughes dies

16 August 1977

ACROSS

1 & 5 Ordinary communal plot or cultivated ground (6,2,6)
9 Listeners who are responsible for a regular balancing act (8)
10 No sham alibi for the cab (6)
12 Not the 19th hole, but players may relax here (5-4)
13 The Spanish snare in Scotland (5)
14 Second-rate request to revel in the sun (4)
16 Point in menace at that place (7)
19 & 21 Weary work for one in service (7,4)
24 Light weight unit spotted at the zoo (5)
25 Ask how Ned prepared for bed in a rough and ready way (5-4)
27 Ring again to rescind the order (6)
28 Turn over a court card when failing to follow suit? (8)
29 There's complication for an *Old Testament* heroine (6)
30 And the rest is spelled out (8)

DOWN

1 & 17 New direction results in soup instead of fish perhaps (6,2,6)
2 Comparatively crazy colouring (6)
3 Frequently decimal (5)
4 Means of securing one involved in a row (7)
6 Humiliation of a dwelling underground (9)
7 Planned to write one's name indeed! . . . (8)
8 . . . otherwise mention a name (8)
11 Put out when time is up (4)
15 Concrete basis for collective total (9)
17 See 1 *down*
18 Goodman and Murphy stick to their decision (5,3)
20 At least partly Oriental (4)
21 Most expensive, darling! (7)
22 Warning: water warmer than 32 degrees Fahrenheit (6)
23 Problem of game scattered about in rising (6)
26 How romantic to fly to an away match! (5)

Elvis Presley dies

18 November 1978

ACROSS

1 Fine feathers are found where the player's cue is awaited (2,3,5)
6 The pick of the fruit (4)
10 Commonly catch the gunners making dried coconut (5)
11 Lacking weight, it brightens the battlefield (4,5)
12 No tears when the landlord isn't paid (4-4)
13 Ground for a broken heart (5)
15 Appeal for little devil with specialised knowledge (7)
17 Muslim ruler takes a little fruit (7)
19 Choose alternatively one who makes his mark in politics (7)
21 A bit in colour for a regular visitor (7)
22 Boy with the French dipper (5)
24 Magnificent rogues go in disarray (8)
27 Incandescent cover for the jet-set? (3,6)
28 Senior of the Spanish and the German (5)
29 Dad's imported yen for profits (4)
30 Describes 24 hours and finish (4,2,1,3)

DOWN

1 Pointless windlass gives short measure (4)
2 Maybe they toil not, but surely they spin, those VIPs? (3,6)
3 Precise instruction to enforce payment (5)
4 Like poetry? Just the opposite (7)
5 Those who ridicule supporters? (7)
7 Beer turns up in royal style (5)
8 Union agent responsible for many a strike (10)
9 Do its members sing only the happy songs? (4,4)
14 Help someone to rise, or forfeit a limb (4,1,3,2)
16 Those summoned to this position rarely find a welcome there (2,3,3)
18 Flabbergasted, due to sand drifting (9)
20 Race row at Henley? (7)
21 In Hades, war breaks up atomic research HQ (7)
23 Irregular study provides a nickname for Miller (5)
25 Turn out Oriental green to the herald (5)
26 Quarrel to become tatty (4)

912 followers of Rev Jim Jones commit suicide

4 May 1979

ACROSS

1 Pat Pluto before going to church and send him away (8)
5 Sort of hats we put bands round (6)
9 Shooting a line about a large reptile and what it can't do? (8)
10 Vulgar civil engineer describing boat propellers (6)
11 Show in puss and stop breathing out! (8)
12 Horrified at being cut by jagged gash (6)
14 One who specialises in doing manual work (10)
18 The dexterity one needs to change into a dress (10)
22 The latest form of stupidity? (6)
23 Step up the number of sappers in action on the flanks? (8)
24 Apparently not a good article on the Persian Gulf (6)
25 Choice piece of beef insufficiently reduced in price? (8)
26 Unprofessional male vocalists? (6)
27 They wield a sinister influence in party politics (8)

DOWN

1 The horse that never let Amelia down (6)
2 Beer that has been diluted and cast out? (6)
3 Change course at the outset and become aggressive (6)
4 Operates a restrictive practice (10)
6 & 19 Misapprehension on the part of the authorities? (8,6)
7 A tortoise I partner badly (8)
8 Toothless old prime minister shown over a famous gallery (8)
13 Notes that conflict? (10)
15 It stops one going off on a flight (8)
16 Motor-cycle race over a sea-girt part of France (8)
17 Assembly of cadgers I put to shame (8)
19 See 6
20 Roman boy turning stuff over to us (6)
21 Ends the sad distress (6)

Thatcher becomes first lady Prime Minister

5 May 1980

ACROSS

1 The water-chute's dry counterpart? (9)
8 Tricky move for a start on board (7,6)
11 Designing part of the foot (4)
12 Small creature, one of a number in a pie (5)
13 Goddess changing her to a bird . . . (4)
16 . . . not a fantail, though it struts with one (7)
17 Account for a broken axle-pin (7)
18 Hold-up in a Hertfordshire town (7)
20 Male preferences? Fair enough (7)
21 Anything but a singular doctrinal link with 7 (4)
22 However you hear it, in honesty you shouldn't (5)
23 The language at Cockney girl's party? (4)
26 When the coast is clear, presumably (2,5,2,4)
27 Pack a gem – it's quite attractive (9)

DOWN

2 Banker giving Florence the go-by (4)
3 Dingy church with a place in modern history (7)
4 Put on a pound and make light of it (7)
5 Lady made an amendment (4)
6 Particular transport causing a stir in places (7,6)
7 There's a moral difference between them (5,3,5)
9 Aid to light concentration (9)
10 Element Agnes and I keep mum about (9)
14 A fine coffee to imitate, one hears (5)
15 Romantic club? (5)
19 Sounded as if the horse made an objection (7)
20 Withdraw with a slipped disc? (4,3)
24 A pound to an old penny one's in next to nothing here (4)
25 Sweet for an aficionado about fifty (4)

SAS storm Iran Embassy freeing 19

29 July 1981

ACROSS

1 Guilt-ridden mole scurrying into fishy dive frequently (9)

9 Clown on an early stage in a swallow-tail (6)

10 Bosses with sea power (9)

11 Exponent of economies OU students link with Milton (6)

12 Poor Alice's let heavenly dwelling (9)

13 More sinister development of broken rule involves GI (6)

17 She gave Long John a leg (3)

19 Where a jog led back to a castle? (7)

20 Gas used to make this conveyance overtake cars (7)

21 Settle back for common chatter (3)

23 Putting together small journal about family relationship (6)

27 Some bloomer if fury follows South African vote (9)

28 Leave by way of early motorway to time (6)

29 Taking the bounce out of an opponent in court? (9)

30 Some sort of sailor, some sort of rascal (6)

31 Motor fuel is able to be transported in it (6,3)

DOWN

2 Comes to life again, given what's beneath top dressing? (6)

3 See, it is given feather tails and tarry (6)

4 A card game of which some vestige turns up over East (6)

5 A teak company redesigned a little table offering (7)

6 Miss front page over booking top model (5,4)

7 Plain-spoken, yes, but this isn't an across clue, OK? (9)

8 Minimum corporal punishment for the junior NCO? (3,6)

14 Period of rising temperatures engendered over witches' cauldron? (4,5)

15 Fearfully friendly type? (9)

16 Can't I lie around dopey first? The very same answer (9)

17 Play without a direct course (3)

18 Opening a doctor round (3)

22 Single-handed seaman first turns out Pearl's mother in a way (7)

24 Dusty playwright? (6)

25 Part of Scotland largely developed without English (6)

26 General Assembly rising to finish a list of things to be done (6)

Charles and Diana's wedding

2 April 1982

ACROSS

1 Surplus wealth? (5,2,5)
8 Capricious mistake I act capriciously about (7)
9 A hundred odd cures for what interest does to an account (7)
11 Dubious character (7)
12 A queue after work of translucent iridescence (7)
13 Lines Jack should know? (5)
14 Designing fellow from the Arctic (9)
16 Nazi VIP describing a blackbird with nowhere to live (9)
19 I held out for foreign capital (5)
21 Futile injunction to cut down waste (7)
23 Give the wrong designation to a grindery holding bills back? (7)
24 The way a river beast turns in quicker time (7)
25 A girl replaced in the Salvation Army (7)
26 Didn't go on supporting different teams? (7,5)

DOWN

1 Raises the price when the exam results are better? (5,2)
2 Spicy things little Margaret gets crazy about (7)
3 The regatta event Cathy arranged to run in? (5,4)
4 Go to a redeveloped part of New Zealand (5)
5 Classical confession of guilt (7)
6 Can rake out only day-to-day work (7)
7 We are free to do whatever we like with them (7,5)
10 A pink pear with high sugar content? (5,7)
15 Bombproof chambers for barristers sharing a brief? (9)
17 A hunter ordered to bring something to light (7)
18 A Merseyside first offender torn to pieces at the finish (7)
19 Swell underworld chief with nurse (7)
20 Workshy bread-makers? (7)
22 On coming in she was radiant (5)

Falklands seized by Argentina

9 June 1983

ACROSS

1 Maybe the idle rich are top when it comes to loafing (5,5)
9 Popular princess or leader in fashion (4)
10 Parent fit enough works in Scottish steel industry (10)
11 Hear sound of machine gun with light infantry ahead (6)
12 Clerical types who invented the steam turbine (7)
15 Perpetual promise of those beauty-aid ads (7)
16 Bird beagle headed off (5)
17 Poky lodgings? (4)
18 Georgia doubly crazy (4)
19 Right in the middle of one's land (5)
21 Light which sends stage manager's hopes up in smoke (3,4)
22 Ted Ray's review has gone off the road (7)
24 To draw a line around a very soft pencil is waste (6)
27 We are apparently unanimous in rejecting an outsider (3,3,2,2)
28 Fever identified in plagues (4)
29 Changes which sent madmen haywire (10)

DOWN

2 Stern nitwit (4)
3 Chest I ransack for rules of conduct (6)
4 Irritating bloomer resulting from traffic queue? (7)
5 American editor briefly employed (4)
6 Culture confined to youth? (7)
7 May be the stomach (6,4)
8 Where to witness a great innings (10)
12 Walker is uninspiringly dull (10)
13 Facing the other way proved to be correct (5,5)
14 Dressing which deserves a dressing down (5)
15 A variety of sole with a bitter taste (5)
19 Song about people in USSR (7)
20 Shocked by a sock (7)
23 Recess for a hundred in love (6)
25 It irritates the sightseer (4)
26 Bankrupt chiseller's representation of top figure (4)

184

Thatcher wins second term

23 April 1984

ACROSS

1 It's material, I'll be bound, on the Medway (10)

6 Capital solo turn (4)

10 & 11 Slightly tipsy, at a pinch? (2,3,5,4)

12 Wastes fried delicacies (8)

13 Delight a serviceman after church (5)

15 Sounds that give colour to the French (7)

17 Craftsman and star in a way (7)

19 Moving home for artist in an Irish county (7)

21 Craft of the local walkabout (7)

22 Shell formerly fly-blown (5)

24 A let-down Sweeney Todd used to advantage (4-4)

27 Means symbols if that is included (9)

28 Stroke of luck baker kneaded (5)

29 Painter of pretty women found in their midst (4)

30 Plastic pass for purchasers (6,4)

DOWN

1 & 14 What an exemplary chap am I. Really! (4,8,2)

2 One not among those up with the lark (4,5)

3 Part of the great liner that is still (5)

4 They carry off rainwater governing head states (7)

5 Where golfers get a magnificent start in Georgia (7)

7 Brilliant type a point ahead (5)

8 Sort of high decoration relevant to the old drawing-room (10)

9 Plant not growing in Cleveland (8)

14 See 1 *down*

16 Bird wide-awake to a current danger on the track (4,4)

18 Thus a pop age provides entertainment (4,5)

20 Smarter French portrait painter (7)

21 Given a build-up to dispel despair (7)

23 Muscle? Could be (5)

25 Piped up for a first public appearance (5)

26 Slip that ends Nanny's charge (4)

AIDS virus identified

1985–94

The late 1980s seemed beset by disasters – both natural and man-made. In 1985 a massive earthquake devastated large parts of Mexico City; a volcano engulfed Armero in Colombia; a cyclone at the mouth of the Ganges caused 10,000 deaths in Bangladesh and the devastating famines in Africa prompted a Live Aid concert in July to raise money for famine relief.

The following year was lightened by the wedding of Prince Andrew and Sarah Ferguson at Westminster. 'Married on a tide of joy' as the *Telegraph* put it on 24 July. The paper went on to say, 'The boost the wedding and associated publicity have given British tourism is probably incalculable.' And for those who couldn't get to England, England was taken to them. The biggest thrash was probably the ball at the Dallas Hotel, Texas . . .

> For guests who could not get enough of the pageantry and human touches of London's big day, the television coverage was replayed throughout the ball on 10ft-high screens.

English chefs and an English pastry cook, recent migrants to Texas, prepared a dinner of roast beef and Yorkshire pudding, Lancashire hot pot and whitebait, with generous quantities of English ale and cider.

The cost of this feast is not recorded.

The 1980s continued its catalogue of disaster: in March 1987, 187 people died when a British ferry, the *Herald of Free Enterprise*, capsized en route to Belgium; and in October, 17 people were killed in the 110 m.p.h. hurricane that swept the south-east of England leaving devastation in the country and red faces in the Meteorological Office whose weathermen had failed to predict it. If anything, 1988 was worse with a horrific fire at the North Sea's Piper Alpha oil rig and the Pan Am Boeing Jumbo jet crashing on Lockerbie in Scotland, just before Christmas, when all the passengers and crew were killed – 255 adults and three children.

These years also saw the advent of the 'new technology'. Computers became involved in the typesetting of newspapers, which meant huge changes at the *Telegraph* and other papers, in some cases involving violent industrial action. The outcome was inevitable and newspaper production entered a new era – and in the *Telegraph*'s case, a new owner. Lord Hartwell sold to Hollinger, and Conrad Black took control of the *Telegraph* in 1986 and soon appointed a new editor, Max Hastings. A year later, the newspaper moved from its traditional site in Fleet Street to a gleaming new building at South Quay in London's revamped Docklands.

This was also a time of huge change within the *Telegraph* crossword: Alan Cash and Tom Pritchard died, and May Abbott retired from compiling. This led to an influx of new blood. Douglas St P. Barnard retained the Monday slot, a very important day in *Telegraph* crossword terms as Monday's issue is likely to be the first one a new reader encounters, and thus the first *Telegraph* crossword he/she will meet – and first impressions, as we all know, matter! Leslie Stokes continued with Tuesday, but a new compiler was brought in to create the Wednesday puzzles. Ann Tait came highly recommended by Douglas St P. Barnard. A teacher and devoted crossword fan, she slotted easily into the house style and was accepted by solvers with no complaint. Ruth Crisp – the doyenne of the crossword compiling world – who created puzzles for all the broadsheets, agreed to take over the Friday crossword and has remained true to the *Telegraph* ever since. Peter Chamberlain started producing the Saturday prize crossword and his puzzles continue to be much enjoyed by solvers during their weekend break.

During this period the way in which crosswords were typeset also changed dramatically. Gone were the printers with their hot-metal, linotype, endless galleys (strips of paper with clues printed on) and final proofs. Gone too were the lead patterns, weighty, 90mm lead squares 22mm deep with a crossword pattern cut into them. As I write, one of them (probably an antique now) acts as a doorstop; it weighs nigh on two kilos! In came a specialized crossword computer program, which automatically makes the correct solution grid and counts the number of letters in each answer to create the numbers in the brackets at the end of each clue. A new era in crossword production was born.

The early 1990s were years when the IRA and its offshoots were carrying out an active bombing programme on the mainland. In 1990 the Stock Exchange was bombed and in 1992 the Baltic Exchange was blown up. Later that year the *Telegraph* moved from South Quay to Canary Wharf, a few hundred metres down the road, where in November that year it had a fortunate escape. In the early evening of Sunday, 15 November, an urgent message came to evacuate the building immediately. It was suspected that a bomb had been planted. It is only due to some observant security men and a faulty detonator that a very unpleasant incident was avoided. On Monday, 16 November, the *Telegraph* appeared with a blank front page and a back page without a crossword. There were complaints from crossword solvers.

During this period Douglas St P. Barnard and Leslie Stokes both became frail and found it increasingly difficult to fulfil their crossword quota. The last of the team I had inherited from Margaret Binstead in 1977 was having its swansong. Various compilers were tried, but none seemed to exactly fit *The Daily Telegraph* template. So, in August 1994 I sought the opinion of the paper's solvers. Six new compilers were used in as many weeks and solvers were invited to assess the puzzles that appeared during this time. Not that *Telegraph* solvers have ever been backward in informing the paper of what they thought of its puzzles. But in this case, I was actively asking their opinion. They duly obliged in a deluge of correspondence and Richard Browne (now editor of *The Times* crossword) was their clear favourite. He took over the regular Tuesday slot on the demise of Leslie Stokes one year later.

Daily Telegraph

No. 40,498. LONDON, FRIDAY, AUGUST 23, 1985   Printed in LONDON and MANCHESTER   23p

Explosion at 100mph

54 DIE IN HOLIDAY JET FIRE

Aborted take-off 'saved lives'

By DAVID GRAVES, STANLEY GOLDSMITH and CHARLES HENRY

FIFTY-FOUR people died and 83 escaped yesterday when a British Airtours Boeing 737 burst into flames as the pilot aborted its take-off for Corfu at Manchester Airport. Two bodies were also burnt.

THATCHER FLIGHT SWITCH

By Our Political Staff

'Scene from hell' in final seconds

By GEORGE TURNBULL

GREENPEACE CASE WOMAN IN ARMY

By John Spooner in Auckland

MAXWELL HALTS 'MIRROR'

By STEPHEN WARD Industrial Staff

Bank holiday trains threat

By MAURICE WEAVER Industrial Staff

Broken turbine burst through fuel pipe

By Air Cdre C. S. COOPER Air Correspondent

INTEREST RATES MAY FALL AGAIN

3 EMERGENCIES IN JAPAN

BANK STRIKE OFF

BAR KILLING

INDEX TO OTHER PAGES

REAGAN BACK IN FIGHTING MOOD

By Our Staff Correspondent in Los Angeles

LATE NEWS

The University of Buckingham

13 July 1985

ACROSS

1 He tries to help; you bet! (7)
5 Says no rubbish at the Pole (7)
9 These two must at least have one! (7)
10 Stealthily goes round for his catches (7)
11 Love to be a producer of oil! (5)
12 Finally, endure the conclusion of a battle (4,5)
13 A Scots girl is mad – goes for one! (7)
14 They pose for artists and are easily shot (7)
16 May be feathered friends of the house proud (7)
19 Made something nothing, to begin with (7)
22 Rank part of a building for learners (9)
24 Is concise in letters, etc (5)
25 Act like a baby on the football field? (7)
26 Going steady? Certainly not! (7)
27 Shorts cuts from these . . . (7)
28 . . . and long for 14 (7)

DOWN

1 A company; one apt to mix food (7)
2 Turns aside, to avoid being stuck in a fight! (7)
3 Ring, eaten? Strangely, something tasty (9)
4 Finishes with the sporting fraternity (7)
5 Rather formal meals (7)
6 Runs along with low interior (5)
7 Get out of the wreck! (7)
8 Tried out in the ship, moves along (7)
15 Enter Matt, upset – so the doctor will give him some of this (9)
16 Scrambled to get information? Quite the opposite (7)
17 Presumably, such power remains (7)
18 Shows hesitation in describing places to wash (7)
19 Came with Academicians, getting pictures from them (7)
20 Insect found in tree with German lunatic (7)
21 Pulls up some of the bed, as it were! (7)
23 Bears off a cutter (5)

Live Aid concert raises £25 million

23 July 1986

ACROSS

1 Given a little rise, as one deserves, when experienced (8)
5 Scouts putting cereal into a vessel (6)
9 Music and dance for taking off? (3-5)
10 Brown's backing the church, showing pluck (6)
11 No longer allowed to include parking, that's clear (8)
12 What may be worn – mink and a couple of rings maybe (6)
14 Judge, a man with a good qualification, meaning degree (10)
18 Principles of study technique (10)
22 Leaves public transport and works (6)
23 General carrying a gun in, concerning an ambassador (8)
24 Sour – makes one twitch (6)
25 Produce notes about the discourse following (8)
26 Cancel the authorisation for a plan? (6)
27 Claim 'X' has been taken in by dreadful creep (8)

DOWN

1 Topping man with constructive ideas (6)
2 A member of a fraternity put out, being short (6)
3 Worked in the open, so excelled (6)
4 Dropped new deal in time (10)
6 Malefactors doubly against one's holding court (8)
7 Sensible bishop's vestment (8)
8 Sailing ship in which sherry may well be served (8)
13 Riches went to provide capital once (10)
15 Cover for a strike-breaker going back far from cheerful (8)
16 Overpowering foreign visitors (8)
17 Carol's going round an animal hospital being critical (8)
19 Lay about everybody as a form of entertainment (6)
20 The girl's taken ill – in a bad way (6)
21 A union measure (6)

Andrew and Fergie marry on a tide of joy

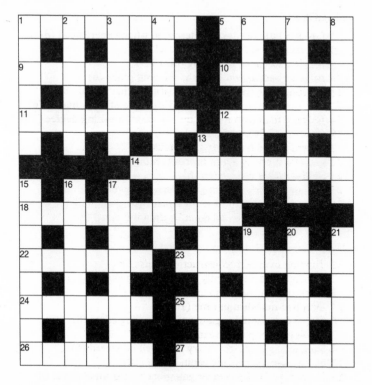

16 October 1987

ACROSS

1 What Jacob did to deceive caused chaos (4,1,4)
9 Silver in the mud? It's an illusion (6)
10 Admit to having had a bath before arrival? (4,5)
11 A lass I wantonly attack (6)
12 Intoxicated now that the wall-covering's on (9)
13 A force of marines in the present era joins a fleet of warships (6)
17 Pinch a little whiskey (3)
19 It's where the winner is initially (2,3,5,5)
20 Flowery tribute from the hospitable island of Hawaii (3)
21 Genuine entertainer doing the rounds of Tyneside (6)
25 Astronomer with a passion for the movies (4-5)
26 Is real novel to be published in instalments? (6)
27 In his bid for success he may study an offer (9)
28 Habit which is not in fashion (6)
29 It's a score settled by outlaw in Athens (9)

DOWN

2 Like to take in tax for the coral islands (6)
3 Very free verse has appeal (4,2)
4 Dusty American playwright (6)
5 They instruct the players about where the coach is going, presumably (5,10)
6 What the city gent wears when cut up? Rubbish! (3-6)
7 Sailing boat is able to move round a Cornish river (9)
8 Story-writers aim to inform (4,5)
14 Corner where the shoe pinches (5,4)
15 All things considered, it may be done slowly or quickly (2,3,4)
16 Sins I came to reform for men's salvation (9)
17 Set-back suffered by a Liberal in love (3)
18 Extra note I added to a letter from Greece (3)
22 Author who is pronouncedly more correct? (6)
23 Can tin alloy produce such an acid? (6)
24 Secluded spot for a vacation (6)

Weathermen fail to predict 110 m.p.h. hurricane

21 December 1988

ACROSS

1 Indifferent to new mural around garden centre (8)
5 Contractions of Wells manuscript (6)
9 Cowardice of leading figure in D-day confusion (8)
10 To be carrying no stress, take a pick-me-up (6)
11 Plane course for late in the day (8)
12 Rare gas in beer or porter (6)
14 Disease of fruit plants can be brief and not serious (4-6)
18 Rook accomplished attack (10)
22 This means being routed another way (6)
23 Swimming race includes part-time soldiers (8)
24 Who is a handsome chap at Oxbridge? (6)
25 VIP? (8)
26 Little Mark reaches maturity in silly infatuation (6)
27 Entire triangle composition (8)

DOWN

1 Account-book with extra line for fiddlers? (6)
2 Fate of a musical show (6)
3 Ghost of war casualty – it appears at hospital (6)
4 Transfer from Real Madrid sometimes caught in net (3-7)
6 Sum of money to swell corporation (3-5)
7 Transported by rail, with green light, for guard duty (6-2)
8 Insurance, for example, gives such peace of mind (8)
13 Smart Londoner leaving bar, drunk (10)
15 Black fake-diamond for a woman slave (8)
16 Underground red bulb (8)
17 Seeing how, for science expedition (8)
19 Wide shot gets the bird . . . (6)
20 . . . but who begins to get bull's eye? Victor! (6)
21 Off-colour? Try a continental spring (6)

Jumbo jet crashes on Lockerbie killing 270

9 November 1989

ACROSS

1 Reached down clumsily for a sovereign (7,4)
10 Main meal has no starter here in 'The Bull' (5)
11 Means of dating a party-dish of grilled meat (9)
12 Pay cashier (9)
13 A Trollope, we hear, retired here in Oklahoma (5)
14 Being rude put bar out (6)
16 Rail-coach worker who threatens the issue? (8)
18 One who complains in car, going round French town (8)
20 Lowest-grade weaver (6)
23 Declare total (5)
24 A girl they moved an immense distance (5-4)
26 Buttercups uncurl in a dance (9)
27 Common stock (5)
28 It takes a turn in presenting Tibetan's petitions (6-5)

DOWN

2 Contacts for bookies' enclosures (5)
3 Main craft of woman with new parish (7)
4 Demand for more from the pit? (6)
5 One takes runners on the road (5-3)
6 Pea lost, somehow, using such a spoon! (7)
7 Disturb canary fluttering at Slimbridge (4,9)
8 It could be set at your place, or mine (5-3)
9 Classical figures LIVID, perhaps (5,8)
15 Hot-rod driving is absolutely fascinating (8)
17 First person in France with a base one in seven! (8)
19 He makes a bit at work – ship is lined with gold (7)
21 Unacceptable charge for fast drainage (7)
22 Hybrid fruit with half of beer is even more horrible (6)
25 Duck will be just out of reach? (5)

Berliners celebrate the fall of the Wall

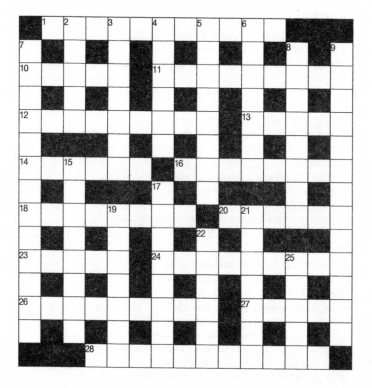

22 November 1990

ACROSS

1 Presidential enthusiasm can set the country alight (4,4)
5 Rex is taken in by a girl? What a jerk! (6)
9 Full board with nobody missing (3,5)
10 A prized metal found around the east from prehistoric times (3-3)
12 Keep sealer in the standard packet (5,4)
13 Scale a trio adapted (5)
14 Sell leather (4)
16 Endeavoured to get about a couple of metres cut (7)
19 Guy goes to village in which Jack retired (7)
21 Books once worn out in Oxford (4)
24 Ponies pass by a back street (5)
25 Good heavens! The incense is burning (4,5)
27 Cretan squash makes a lovely drink (6)
28 Overcome the stigma of being a basement tenant (4,4)
29 A continent and pure old English composition (6)
30 Let India be prepared with all the facts (2,6)

DOWN

1 Cook for trains on first-class Chunnel link route (6)
2 Sarah gets depressed and rather jaundiced (6)
3 Loud pop music becomes a habit (5)
4 Standing for election and apparently canvassing enthusiastically (7)
6 Looking about (9)
7 Late arriving in Scotland – around midday (8)
8 Argued, and with great fluency (3,5)
11 What the conductor should do best (4)
15 Hurry to give the appearance of cleverness (4,5)
17 No chance to work up a dance (8)
18 Mini auto as opposed to an automobile (5,3)
20 One hears of the old king who reunited Germany (4)
21 Total sum no one raised – except maybe the chancellor (7)
22 Travel in refurbished boat to South American capital (6)
23 Herb Hutton returned to the marsh (6)
26 Footsie generally included investment (5)

Thatcher quits as Prime Minister

16 January 1991

ACROSS

1 Drink with little hesitation, so get fatter! (7)
5 Stays, but desires to move (7)
9 Page respecting nurse's claim (7)
10 Gave way and took photographs (7)
11 Playing tennis – it's demanding (9)
12 Quiet trainee making a stand (5)
13 Some of the more menacing rebels get the bird (5)
15 Where to pull a hundred trees out (9)
17 Talk of the devil and run! (9)
19 An old book to piece together (5)
22 Dance music for 27 to some degree (5)
23 He'll take no alcohol – may order tea in bars (9)
25 Giving a name to one's business (7)
26 Striking fashion causing shock (7)
27 Foreign holy man needing cattle-grazing (7)
28 7? That's serious (7)

DOWN

1 Digging can be tiring (7)
2 Boss is through with the episcopate (7)
3 Rows involving joiners (5)
4 Rubicund character of some importance (3-6)
5 Once again put to sleep without point (5)
6 *New Testament* account (9)
7 Settle the down-payment (7)
8 Skilled worker getting more depressed about the Left (7)
14 No-one thanks a fellow for turning up and calling out (9)
16 This could well give some edge to the news broadcast (9)
17 Exercises control over charges (7)
18 Like the gentleman receiving junk mail (7)
20 Set time allowed for dressing (7)
21 Persons in the wrong environment, and suffering as a result (7)
23 Fish caught in an Arcadian glen (5)
24 Moving article on prison (5)

Air strikes against Iraq begin

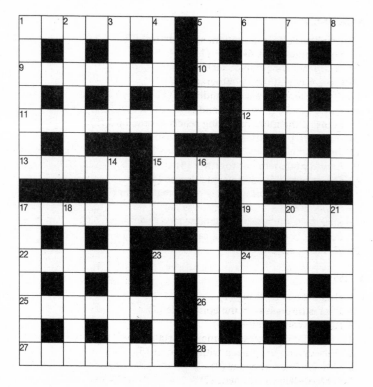

11 November 1992

ACROSS

1 Settle down to write notes personally (7,7)
9 Ape should achieve rapid growth (4,3)
10 Disorderly mess left in a sailing ship (7)
11 Set out to follow a small car (4)
12 To fall out is offensive during short vacations (5,5)
14 English join forces and come into the open (6)
15 Took great pains to diagnose disorder (8)
17 A penny-pincher about to acquire a spray (8)
18 A vessel has trouble mounting attack (6)
21 Hostile to MI6? Just the opposite (10)
22 Crow moulded out of British silver (4)
24 His commission is to set the work-place right (7)
25 Rise and dress (4,3)
26 Give way to lenient Scandinavians in church (2,7,5)

DOWN

1 Minor cleric admits time must be reduced (3-4)
2 Force the doctors to adapt and exploit the situation (4,3,4,2,2)
3 Its player would love to be held in honour (4)
4 Struggle to overturn iron citadel (6)
5 Free the suspect! (2,6)
6 Conservative views on what constitutes an equilateral rectangle (10)
7 To unfasten locks is to throw caution to the winds (3,4,4,4)
8 Rudely enquired about small purchase made (6)
13 Selfish, spoilt socialite without gravity (10)
16 Presenting Anglican theology lessons to Birmingham requires some brain (8)
17 The flower of warring womanhood (6)
19 A note taken in by members of the embassy (7)
20 Pay attention and be silent in form (6)
23 For Penny it's a stimulus (4)

Church of England votes for women priests

29 July 1993

ACROSS

1 Harassed doctor went into digs outside (9)
9 No mail going into this distant depot? (7)
10 Request border with earth and soil (7)
11 In which cold sheets are thrown off? (3,4)
12 Ship's crew below with utter ease (5,4)
14 Parasite ready-made for baiting? (8)
15 War-zone violation, opening ammunition (6)
17 He will applaud a bell-ringer (7)
20 Long a feature of Chesterfield – praise be – twisted! (6)
23 Hobo mien may produce easy good nature (8)
25 Wait outside coach, according to law (9)
26 Individual turning sour can be burdensome (7)
27 Accountant advances money on the first of every month no longer (7)
28 Costly, the French article that supports 20? (7)
29 Shabby condition of side – sense a change? (9)

DOWN

2 O, write a song of the great outdoors! (4,3)
3 Flatness of colour in a long beam (7)
4 Army regiment laid up – for such treatment? (8)
5 Man in a mask – double one, for example (6)
6 They run starkers, wantonly, about the end of June (9)
7 Muscle that moves up and down? No, about an axis (7)
8 Draw at Maltese resort (9)
13 Beat favourite dog (7)
15 Where people meet after putting hammer on line (9)
16 He comport clumsily as a light, delicate sort? (9)
18 A steward travelling to the orient (8)
19 Whole number, for example, in Bury (7)
21 Neat bird model (7)
22 Red rose embroidered for the choir-screen (7)
24 Topics of children on Sunday? (6)

Stephen Lawrence murder suspects freed

10 May 1994

ACROSS

7 Skeleton service? (4,5)
8 Test for car or engine (5)
10 A train driver (8)
11 No traffic is met in such a street (3,3)
12 Go ahead with a new deal (4)
13 Musical instrument untouched (8)
15 Rough-looking punk met with violence (7)
17 Cut off, and also tie off (7)
20 Toothsome vegetable – grown only for decoration (5,3)
22 Trendy accountant was found in Peru (4)
25 Pole position? (6)
26 Highly attractive part of Belgium (8)
27 Vegetable has one on both sides (5)
28 Port of fine quality (9)

DOWN

1 The bosun is out to make extra money (5)
2 Strict clergyman turns up in the diocese (6)
3 Animal disinfectant mixed deep inside the vessel (8)
4 A stroke by a batsman, going for a run perhaps? (2,5)
5 Makings of a mountain? (8)
6 One tap-bar drunk may think himself Napoleon (9)
9 Time to do a hand's turn (4)
14 Responding to a phone call about disturbing news (9)
16 Emergency exit for a pilot (8)
18 There's a certain wildness in such devious dealings (8)
19 Dash to get article into cheap production (7)
21 Wolves forwards playing Rugby (4)
23 Stick around at home like a dog (6)
24 Finish with conclusion of judge in lawsuit (5)

Mandela becomes South Africa's president

1995–2005

In the mid-1990s *The Daily Telegraph* D-Day crosswords affair was resurrected once again. The compiler at the centre of the cause célèbre had been headmaster of the Strand School and, as such, his portrait had been painted. Over the years the school had changed and relocated, and the portrait had been relegated to a dusty corner. The school's Old Boys' association decided to offer the portrait to the *Telegraph*, which was delighted to receive it. By way of thanks the newspaper hosted a lunch for some of the oldest members of the association. Inevitably, the D-Day crossword affair was the main topic of conversation and was discussed with a passion that was quite remarkable, given that the events had been some 50 years earlier. It was very pleasant to spend a lunchtime reminiscing about crosswords compiled during a war long gone, and escape the realities of the present day.

When looking at the headlines of this ten-year period, it is impossible not to see it as a decade of mayhem and terror. In 1995, a government office building in Oklahoma was blown apart by the American terrorist

Timothy McVeigh, and the Israeli prime minister was shot dead by an Israeli terrorist. The following year the *Telegraph*'s previous home in Docklands, South Quay, was blown up by IRA terrorists, signalling the end of the cease-fire agreement, and Manchester's city centre was ripped out by another IRA bomb.

The reality is that these headlines only reflect a tiny percentage of what happens around us, but because they are unusual events, they become the news stories that hit the headlines. The vast majority of what happens is not newsworthy – it is far less dramatic. Occasionally, such events find their way into the lower columns of a newspaper – particularly if they are a trifle bizarre. Such was the case of the 'crossword will' reported in 1999.

Anetta Duel had died at the age of 99 and her family could find no will. However, her nephew found a scrawled message – in which she left him all her worldly possessions – written on the side of a *Daily Telegraph* crossword. The trouble was that the will was not dated, and that is where *The Daily Telegraph*'s crossword office swung into action. With a very efficient filing system, it was quite easy to track down the date when the crossword in question had been printed – each crossword has a number and can therefore be traced back to its original date. Lawyers confirmed that, since it was properly signed, Mrs Duel's rather unusual-looking will did not have to be witnessed by a third party. The size of the estate was not disclosed.

This little story appeared not only in the *Telegraph* but was wired around the world. It led to my being contacted by the National Puzzle Museum on the south shores of Lake Erie in the United States. Being interested in all things to do with puzzles and crosswords, they wanted details of both the Duel 'will' story and the D-Day crossword clues story. So a little bit of *The Daily Telegraph* crossword's history is alive and well and living in Ohio.

The millennium rolled to its conclusion, its final year seeing the Columbine High School massacre in the United States, Jonathan Aitken going to jail, a total eclipse of the sun, an East Anglian farmer being arrested for killing a young burglar, and the fiasco of the Millennium Dome at Greenwich. As cryptic crossword solvers know (being sticklers for accuracy), one of the most irritating aspects of the whole millennium celebration was that it was not the end of the millennium, which did not occur until the end of the year 2000. However, bowing to the inevitable, *The Daily Telegraph* printed its biggest ever crossword on Saturday, the first of January 2000. With 226 clues and a 45x45 square pattern, it was a monster puzzle – sadly not in this book as it is far too large to fit. The £1,000 prize was won by a lady from Cheadle Heath near Stockport.

It would be impossible write anything about the years so far in this new millennium without referring to the events of 11 September 2001. More than anything they defined the age in which we now live. By an eerie coincidence a crossword compiler of my acquaintance had that day created a giant puzzle in which solvers would have filled in these solutions:

```
        W
        O
        R
        L
        D
        T
        R
        A
        D
      J E T
        C
        E
        N
        T
        R
        E
```

An extraordinary coincidence but one with which most crossword editors are familiar.

The Fortean Times – the magazine specializing in the world of strange phenomena – has featured *The Daily Telegraph*'s crossword more than once. There was, of course, the D-Day crossword clues affair, but also a crossword that mentioned the name of a ferry and its captain a week before the ferry capsized – with loss of life – in the North Sea (it was not the Zeebrugge disaster).

Extraordinary coincidences are one of the banes of a crossword editor's life. I well remember going on holiday for three weeks in July 1990 (all the crosswords having been duly set in advance) to return to a furore over a single cryptic crossword clue – and a very good clue it was:

Clue: Outcry at Tory assassination (4,6)
Solution: *Blue murder*

Unfortunately, it appeared on the day when the front page was totally devoted to the IRA's assassination of Ian Gow, the Conservative MP. The clue had been created some four months previously, edited six weeks before and entered in the *Telegraph*'s computer before I went on holiday. It was just a terrible coincidence, but one I never forgot. It may be hard to credit, but one of my duties as crossword editor is to check the following day's crossword against the evening news bulletins – just to look out for unfortunate coincidences – and when I go on holiday a night news sub-editor takes over the task.

In January 2003, Richard Browne's last puzzle appeared in *The Daily Telegraph* – he had been appointed crossword editor to *The Times* (trouble is, of course, that the *Telegraph* trains them so well!). His Tuesday slot was taken by Anne Campbell Dixon whose main occupation is writing heritage articles, but she finds time to both create and sub-edit crossword puzzles.

The final crossword in this book epitomizes how far the *Telegraph* crossword has travelled in its 80-year history. You might consider reacquainting yourself with the puzzle that was first printed on 30 July 1925, before tackling this final puzzle. This addictive pastime has occupied an important place in the pages of *The Daily Telegraph* for 80 years and with up to 20,000 entries wa week to the paper's Saturday prize crossword and a bulging post bag from interested solvers every week, I see no reason why it should not be celebrating its 100th birthday in 2025. Will it get a telegram from the monarch, I wonder? After all, it is believed the current queen is a fan.

Happy solving!

Front page from 1995

2 December 1995

ACROSS

1 Sweet girl goes after the fruit (5,9)
9 Remarkable master, I concluded, amongst masters of an art (7)
10 Again thanks boy who had been caught again (7)
11 Promising girl (4)
12 Considerate, but not empty-headed? (10)
14 Make a casual visit on physician doing small operation at home (4,2)
15 Double-first (4-4)
17 Deserter had gold deficiency first! (8)
18 Agree to trick the dog (6)
21 Ropy clothing? (6,4)
22 Curious lust of an immoral woman (4)
24 Where to spend time underground (7)
25 Discharge coming from polluted lake before time (7)
26 Didn't one keep one's cool in this dispute? (6,8)

DOWN

1 Had high opinion of another maid, left-winger (7)
2 Squeeze pear during the interview (5,10)
3 Met tyrant trapping artist (4)
4 Measure up (6)
5 Gave directions a different way? (8)
6 Many-sided figure anchored to go adrift (10)
7 Go without saying (4,6,5)
8 Chain surrounding low joint (6)
13 Disturb record formerly right (10)
16 Constance and archdeacon Edward came together (8)
17 Do nothing about Sidney dancing back to back (4-2)
19 Beat it! (7)
20 New roles about time for one working in the stables (6)
23 Tag is acceptable although forbidden (4)

Rogue trader Nick Leeson jailed for fraud

10 February 1996

ACROSS

1 One succeeds without trying (9)
6 Is this what the filthy rich possess? (5)
9 Loud suit for party (7)
10 All the same how soldiers should dress (9)
11 Remarkably not a river in Spain but a lake in America (7)
12 Originate from gentleman at embassy (7)
13 Hints coming during stormy weather? (6,2,3,4)
18 Well-read clergymen? (7)
20 Thanks graduates taking care of the hot pepper sauce (7)
22 Churchman who operates a restraining influence? (9)
23 Mark one hundredth piece (7)
24 Poles in river found a yellow-flowered plant (5)
25 Not time to be tough! (6,3)

DOWN

1 At home celebrated being notoriously vile! (8)
2 Pedlar stuck with her in trouble (8)
3 I read about rebel leader, an attacker (6)
4 Sustained on the piano perhaps (6)
5 Kind of square diet first for the soldiers (8)
6 Drink article featured in French newspaper (8)
7 Unlawful act on a Ukrainian peninsula (6)
8 Last letter to enemy about protein substance produced by cells (6)
14 Shipping lane? (8)
15 Train Rita to drop a bothersome nuisance (8)
16 I sing in a medley about badges of office (8)
17 One cannot perform this in play (8)
18 Fight medico in a jacket (6)
19 An ecclesiastical dignitary from the mountains (6)
20 No trap set for fish (6)
21 Go briskly and cheerily along in the light wind (6)

Deep Blue defeats Kasparov at chess

1 May 1997

ACROSS

1 Set antidotes may be called for (9)
9 Commentary by an upright journalist? (6)
10 The pedagogue travelled on in a very bad way (9)
11 Chance getting the wind up about the doctor (6)
12 Large animals make less noise (9)
13 Coppers following a skilled man (6)
17 Tea specially prepared for a Greek character (3)
19 'Behold, Esau my —— is a hairy man . . .' (*Bible*) (7)
20 Caught and being tried for causing a fight (7)
21 Dine in the home at 7.30 (3)
23 Judge upstart politician with some displeasure (6)
27 Enters and makes an impression (9)
28 Roofing of the church specified (6)
29 Maintain ministers should set the scene (9)
30 The more disagreeable serving man? (6)
31 Show material to view with distaste (9)

DOWN

2 It's possibly about a man's dissertation (6)
3 It's exhausting dressing (6)
4 The most aged and most chilly – about to drop off (6)
5 Section of the Spanish and French taking people in (7)
6 Coming to and bearing with everything involved (9)
7 A personal toaster (9)
8 Combine badly-treating Oriental (9)
14 Revolutionary order given to a military body (5,4)
15 An ailment of grouse (9)
16 Figure perhaps he's just idiosyncratic (9)
17 Showing some hesitation over a certain point before (3)
18 Bill's work (3)
22 Moderate hail-storm (7)
24 He'll beat the drink soundly! (6)
25 Makes no progress in the market (6)
26 Read about mould required for a spectacular pot-plant (6)

Labour routs Tories in election

26 January 1998

ACROSS

1 Resent having to accept second said thing that doesn't follow general rule (4,9,2)
9 What, say, flower was uprooted by birds swimming? (9)
10 Have only a fraction of a body of constables (5)
11 Move about the home (7)
12 A live TV broadcast in Israel (3,4)
13 Regret cruel heart (3)
14 Fellow with Sally 'e intercepted wrongly (7)
17 Fit in the German inhabitant (7)
19 Cap that is not worn on one's head (7)
22 The romp round a place in Northumberland (7)
24 The French article in the open country (3)
25 Term Lee devised for a tall plant (3-4)
26 It is possible to calm down the queen in the story (7)
28 Fare needed to board a bus perhaps (3,2)
29 Sound as a bell (4-1-4)
30 Move clumsily with a pair of like measures (4,3,4,4)

DOWN

1 Powerful tug that can be relied on (5,2,8)
2 Drawing all but the top of the boat (5)
3 Along the way in France? (2,5)
4 Falsify accounts with fifth rate lines, it's done in the kitchen (7)
5 Guided polite members to front door (7)
6 Sudden decision of one Frenchman on the beat (7)
7 Dandy serf not in music city (9)
8 Intoxicated cox? (3,4,3,5)
15 Left one composing motet outside before four with recurring theme (9)
16 Lady from Long Island going to mid-Wales (3)
18 Try to win affection in court (3)
20 Title a Brontë could have arranged (7)
21 Most of the charged particle used on the printing plate (7)
22 Coat for baby in afternoon performance (7)
23 Batter some defence (7)
27 Main water supply (5)

Clinton denies affair with Monica Lewinsky

11 August 1999

ACROSS

1 Sun block from Europe borders on second best (7)
5 They are often cast as followers (7)
9 Reign disrupted by ship's arrival (7)
10 Sign of a fashionable food additive (7)
11 Ignorant tinker had need of translation (2,3,4)
12 I would start to ignore books – fool! (5)
13 Ex-PM's point (5)
15 One's carried traverse to green, somehow (9)
17 Are they duty bound? Hardly! (9)
19 Reduce water supply to queen (5)
22 Be all at sea, though on the case (5)
23 The sweet music of a Vatican drummer? (5,4)
25 Empty cell – fury at error! (7)
26 Metaphors from lines by one wise man (7)
27 Peter's changed round Colin's initial view (7)
28 Scored – gallery in agreement (7)

DOWN

1 Issue diet plan with no-one's backing (7)
2 Vessel that could be fired (7)
3 Exercise first mate found an annoyance (5)
4 Mushy peas, say, – that's simple (4,2,3)
5 Suddenly starting to pay attention to the conman (5)
6 Sober, can enter – not here (9)
7 Thinking of nothing, and missing badly (7)
8 What to wear and set off this? (7)
14 Stress that drunk is not heavy (9)
16 A small quantity might give grounds for arrest (9)
17 Picks the groups that take in the Spanish (7)
18 University doctor's anger at offence (7)
20 Object to rubbish being taken in by nuisance (7)
21 About to take a bet on editor, but passed it on (7)
23 Odds about early start to drinking bout (5)
24 Quiet at the back, Rod! (5)

Millions marvel at total eclipse

1 January 2000

ACROSS

7 Quite drunk, all knocked back a second – of these? (9)

8 On sub perhaps he is in charge on the seas (5)

10 Turn tense after scare about edible snail (8)

11 List sailor's condition, a little bit frail (6)

12 Large hairy monster that's still on the isle (4)

13 For example, in people you'll witness denial (8)

15 Feathers on hat held by messenger, say (7)

17 Chatterers' epigrams cracked right away (7)

20 Soldiers retreating with man coming out (8)

22 Cries inconsolably, boss being about (4)

25 A part of a church for which one has yen (6)

26 Note, fool with a letter to look at again (8)

27 Persian neighbour, a witch in a story that's Greek (5)

28 Volume of poetry found on this peak? (9)

DOWN

1 Stab English eccentric, a man with no feeling (5)

2 For poison a recipe comes into healing (6)

3 Beating your crewmen, illicitly selling (8)

4 Rules about junction where Swiss folk are dwelling (7)

5 Dogs, say, cross over for a thick slice of bread (8)

6 Run into sick nurse one's found in a bed (9)

9 What you may shoot when guns turn around? (4)

14 Spots Miss Hebe with student inextricably bound (9)

16 Cables with damages, accepting a note (8)

18 Sailor makes mark but refuses to vote (8)

19 Girl clutches bird on a part of her chest (7)

21 Eastern retreat, where no-one was dressed (4)

23 A saint in the highest? No, lowest I am! (6)

24 Quietly sends up what's owed for a sham (5)

World celebrates new millennium

11 September 2001

ACROSS

1 Acting Shakespeare's first what's-his-name (6)
5 P-position for a sentimental regard (4,4)
9 German tenor turned out nice (8)
10 What hung on wicked stepmothers' wall-paper? (6)
11 Design of furniture for North Sea trip (8)
12 Sign of twin brothers we look up to (6)
13 Turner's work left, following extreme torment, on lawn? (8)
15 She, a naval architect? (4)
17 High peaks climbed whilst holding record (4)
19 I, Pandora worried with delusions of grandeur (8)
20 Shock, finding university in a backward trading-centre (6)
21 Excited uncertainty of American writers in south-east (8)
22 English team were in front, having been sent abroad (6)
23 A cat is approaching the queen? Spray needed! (8)
24 Guard is despatched to new line (8)
25 Drunkenly sat on a form used by Beethoven (6)

DOWN

2 Accomplished try to eavesdrop (8)
3 Hazel could be such a brunette (8)
4 Long-term hospitals for treatment of aortas in a mess (9)
5 This is not the winning post (6-5,4)
6 Spear free while camping (7)
7 Standard is raised over river in opera (8)
8 Expression in America for a boundary marker (8)
14 They help us to walk after a heavy fall (9)
15 She might serve woman with first-class braid of hair (8)
16 Chinese white, for example? (8)
17 Union somehow had row overturned (8)
18 Outlook for a possible customer (8)
19 One that is standing up to grandeur in ancient city (7)

Terrorists destroy the World Trade Center

30 March 2002

ACROSS

1 One of the family is boarding (7)
5 Regain health but take out extra insurance? (7)
9 Add something – a grated nutmeg possibly (7)
10 Express this in a single sentence! (3-4)
11 A fleshy-leaved plant producing weighty harvest (9)
12 Critical about hard though most suitable position (5)
13 A supplement is for the recess (5)
15 Gifts of iron hoops (9)
17 Unduly put out when in charge of the children (9)
19 It's worth making time about mid-afternoon (5)
22 Employees getting support (5)
23 A restorer dealing with furniture for storage (9)
25 Out in the arena inflicting defeat (7)
26 Area where one keeps changing gear (7)
27 Choose gold for a royal personage (7)
28 Listening equipment may be sent, and that's serious (7)

DOWN

1 Port holds the western answer in the main (7)
2 Copy to rivet attention (7)
3 The setting for some confrontation (5)
4 No rocky situation – before debts become widely known (9)
5 Speedily made an artist joke mounts (3,2)
6 A firm sister beat the problem (9)
7 Church authority in the forefront at one hundred (7)
8 Soldiers stand over the crowd and keep under control (7)
14 He objects to laying out money for a hide of stone (9)
16 A bird taken as picnic food? (9)
17 Verbose characters, say (7)
18 Total wipe-out is certain after a time (7)
20 Stood up and scoffed, looking quite pink (7)
21 To let a thousand in can cause distress (7)
23 A jolly fellow no longer up the pole – at sea (5)
24 Appear hesitant, right or wrong (5)

Queen Mother dies

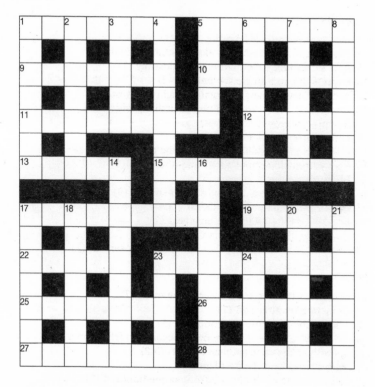

24 May 2003

ACROSS

1 Small person's wife going into spasm (6)
4 How healthy pig will go the full extent? (5,3)
10 Not starting to be less hairy tree! (5)
11 Lover in foreign capital returning a word of thanks (9)
12 Term very much like another (7)
13 Watches initial part of poster be put at the end (7)
14 Policy is to ask for money – at a premium? (9,5)
17 Cover used during one's retirement designed piecemeal (9,5)
21 Find Lee struggling in the London area (7)
23 Rachel Flint's middle name, we hear – oh, well! (5-2)
24 Musical folder? (9)
25 Club may charge (5)
26 A beading removed whilst producing banter (8)
27 Main trade route (6)

DOWN

1 Pierce through vehicles I left for repair (8)
2 No aides in developing country (9)
3 He will investigate if anyone is unusually late (7)
5 Hating research about examination of one's deepest feelings (5-9)
6 Heraldic beast, once ill, sickens (7)
7 Lift to interminable place of happiness (5)
8 In spring Dan skied in Poland (6)
9 Union members celebrate it after over half a century (7,7)
15 Dish causing turmoil in the Emerald Isle? (5,4)
16 Lawyer's power? (8)
18 Band opposing Ronald, revolutionary leader (7)
19 Queen on river did not start to argue over petty things (7)
20 Smear be over a bud developing (6)
22 Fellow with daughter accepted one resisted (5)

244

Eurovision Song Contest won by Turkey

3 July 2004

ACROSS

1 Patient and has been for some time? (4-9)
9 Do not forget to hold another meeting (9)
10 At home with most of the money as a joke (2,3)
11 Jane included single nest (5)
12 Group will go North of the Border (4)
13 Part horse, part god (4)
15 Moving goods are in it (7)
17 More involved with the preceding principle? (7)
18 Song about rotter in ancient Greece (7)
20 Follow after flourish (7)
21 Tribal leader getting nothing in return for cotton (4)
22 Extremely nervous? (4)
23 Could provide power (5)
26 Long and thin fellow first in the side (5)
27 Bright fish taking single insect (9)
28 Soft-centred kind (6-7)

DOWN

1 Like an overdrawn fictional character? (6-4-4)
2 New rice pudding more attractive (5)
3 Joint Argentine XI (10)
4 Her gift transported as cargo (7)
5 Old can caught dead (7)
6 I offer to be in the same place (4)
7 Forget his remarkable equine present! (4,5)
8 One French salesman falsely thought it had not been studied
   beforehand (14)
14 Chapel beam redirected onto fruit dish (5,5)
16 On the way up to position of eminence (9)
19 Build a monstrosity on the point – that's clear (7)
20 Such prices have reached the ceiling and beyond (3-4)
24 Organ transplant is hard work (5)
25 It covers all of us all the time (4)

17-year-old Russian girl wins Wimbledon

30 July 2005

ACROSS

1 Common party in which joints are presented, alternately, to guests (5-2)
5 Put another coat on (7)
9 Looks at with an expression of friendliness (7)
10 Wycliffite uplifted everyone in the name of Christ (7)
11 ———— (9)
12 New colour (5)
13 Where the plane crashed in a mountainous country (5)
15 Male tutors go round first – pleasure's their sole objective (9)
17 ———— (9)
19 Physician in good health upset design (5)
22 Network a French city originated (5)
23 Leading figure giving new life to others (9)
25 ———— (7)
26 Fiery soldier getting up with commonsense going round the point (7)
27 Without breaks is no French way to work (7)
28 This sort of party can get one really strung up! (7)

DOWN

1 Nail-hardener carried by tanker at Inverness (7)
2 Urge to toss a drink (3-4)
3 Neck of rugged rock to the South (5)
4 Hip-coat is altered for a nut (9)
5 Name for the trainee in harp-construction (5)
6 Go in river Lyn with Greek character who comes back with buckwheat (9)
7 Disorderly place to find an orderly (2,1,4)
8 News of rises and falls in sea level? (7)
14 The boor interrupted by a woman's attacks (6,3)
16 Discount the inference (9)
17 Understand how to become popular (5,2)
18 Nevertheless he may be a member of a brotherhood (4,3)
20 Remove house-bound wife's cause for complaint (4,3)
21 Divine appropriate to English diocese (7)
23 Settle your debts now that there has been a wage rise (3,2)
24 Crazy as one can get from an iced drink (5)

Solvers create clues for Telegraph puzzle

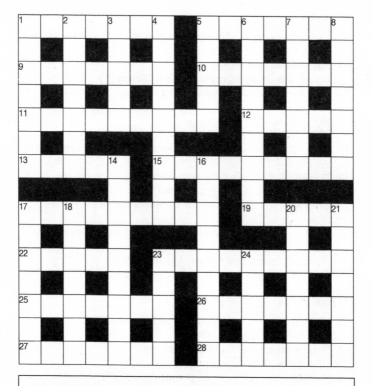

The omission of three clues from this puzzle (two nine-letter words and one seven-letter word) is not a mistake but a deliberate exclusion to be rectified by the one component of *The Daily Telegraph* crossword's success that, so far, has not been mentioned – you, the solver. Without the hundreds of thousands of avid *Telegraph* crossword solvers the puzzle would have been what was originally intended – a six-weeks diversion – but your enthusiasm over the years has ensured it a permanent place in the newspaper. The three solution words omitted can be deduced from the content of this book. Compile your own clue for one, two or all these solution words and send them – together with your name, address and phone number – to the address listed with the solution to this puzzle at the back of the book. The best clues will be included in the birthday puzzle (different to this one) to be published in *The Daily Telegraph* on Saturday, 30 July 2005.

SOLUTIONS

1925

ACROSS

1 Byron
5 Poe
8 X-rays
13 Raid
14 Drake
16 Arum
17 Aloe
18 Raker
19 Pile
20 Nets
21 OM
22 So
23 Tael
25 Swim
28 Lop
30 Balm
34 Spot
35 Romeo
37 Soit
39 Oar
40 Corunna
41 Inn
42 List
44 Bilge
45 Bret
46 Neat
47 Sue
48 Beer
53 Agag
57 OC
59 ie
60 Acre
63 Mace
64 Crete
66 Plan
67 Etna
68 Harem
69 Sort
70 Seers
71 Gem
72 Medes

DOWN

1 Brand
2 Yale
3 Riot
4 Odes
5 Pram
6 Oak
7 Ekes
9 Rapt
10 Aria
11 Yule
12 Smelt
14 Drop
15 Eros
24 Romulus
25 Spain
26 Worse
27 It
28 Loris
29 Penge
31 As
32 Loire
33 Miner
34 Sol
35 Rob
36 One
38 TNT
43 Ta
45 Be
49 James
50 Hoch
51 Deem
52 Dents
54 Gate
55 Acne
56 Gear
58 Crag
59 Item
60 Apse
61 Clod
62 Rare
65 Ere

1926

ACROSS

1 Interchangeable
9 Tidings
11 Bluecap
13 Greases
14 Rood
16 Clue
17 Leans
19 Creel
20 Reel
21 Thorn
22 Nisi
23 Team
25 Coati
27 Adit
29 Sight
30 Ennui
31 Rest
32 Ramc
33 Troikas
37 Himself
38 Initial
39 Pusillanimously

DOWN

1 Interpretership
2 Tadpole
3 Rung
4 Hose
5 Nibs
6 Emus
7 Bacilli
8 Euphemistically
10 Grant
12 Learn
15 Delimit
16 Centaur
18 Shoot
19 Crate
24 Assumes
25 Churl
26 Inman
28 Diaries
33 Teal
34 Offa
35 Kiwi
36 Silo

1927 1928 1929

1927

ACROSS

1 Harass
5 Sippet
8 Plantagenet
12 Bure
13 Shire
14 Drop
15 Ferrara
17 Babel
19 Gland
21 Amuse
22 Lyric
23 Oates
24 Other
25 Inter
27 Azure
28 Spode
29 Nerve
31 Retired
35 Abel
37 Mined
38 Gust
39 Responsions
40 Whinny
41 Tether

DOWN

1 Hubbub
2 Able
3 Sense
4 Chair
5 Sheer
6 Pied
7 Torpid
8 Probationer
9 Three
10 Grail
11 Treacherous
15 Fluster
16 Aground
18 Emend
20 Litre
26 Ratio
27 Acres
28 Shadow
30 Esther
32 Empty
33 Inner
34 Edict
36 Lean
38 Gnat

1928

ACROSS

1 Knight Errants
10 Overlap
11 Florida
12 Seldom
15 Settle
16 Parlour
17 Nose
18 Herd
19 Giraffe
20 Undo
22 Acts
24 Heretic
26 Nectar
27 Toledo
30 Triumph
31 Utilize
32 Merry Thoughts

DOWN

2 Needles
3 Gallop
4 Type
5 Rife
6 Adorer
7 Thistle
8 Consanguinity
9 Kaleidoscopes
13 Mariner
14 Bloater
15 Surfeit
21 Decline
23 Cheviot
24 Hammer
25 Coping
28 Whet
29 Hugo

1929

ACROSS

1 Trafalgar
9 Geneva
10 Spirit
11 Haul
12 Malaga
13 Retriever
15 Rue
16 Square
19 Let
21 Awkward
22 Utensil
24 Sag
26 Impede
29 Tab
31 Ptarmigan
32 Labour
34 Lute
35 Caribs
36 Toilet
37 Ascension

DOWN

2 Rapier
3 Furore
4 Litter
5 Athlete
6 Velasquez
7 Zenana
8 Bagatelle
9 Gum
14 Tuck
17 Vacillate
18 Landaulet
19 LDS
20 Tug
23 Stag
25 Artless
27 Public
28 Crèche
29 Tigris
30 Bamboo
33 Rut

1930   1931   1932

1930

ACROSS

3 Basis
8 Mohair
9 Treble
10 Poplin
11 Fandango
12 Era
13 Dorset
14 Cracknel
17 Unfeted
19 Begging
23 Trumpery
27 Merlin
29 Pea
30 Cucumber
31 Nankin
32 Celery
33 Equity
34 Ousel

DOWN

1 Rococo
2 Carlisle
3 Brunette
4 Surface
5 Stanza
6 Remark
7 Plague
13 Doubt
15 Cog
16 Logan
18 Top
20 Emmanuel
21 Geranium
22 Cypress
24 Reuben
25 Mauser
26 Embryo
28 Idiots

1931

ACROSS

1 Satanic
5 Bicycle
9 Liszt
10 Rusticate
11 Homer
12 Cymbeline
14 Ida
15 Ratio
16 Brisket
19 Behests
22 Catch
24 Hue
25 Garibaldi
29 Skimp
30 Treadmill
31 Agate
32 Ideally
33 Withers

DOWN

1 Sulphur
2 Test Match
3 Notorious
4 Curacao
5 Besom
6 Clive
7 Coati
8 Everest
13 Bar
17 Incessant
18 Kittiwake
19 Bugatti
20 Tea
21 Whitlow
23 Hapless
26 Reeve
27 Bedel
28 Laity

1932

ACROSS

1 Patrolling
6 Calf
10 Nymph
11 Registrar
12 Gruesome
13 Hawse
15 Stipend
17 Toddler
19 Raeburn
21 Dolphin
22 Nyasa
24 Environs
27 Masterful
28 Jorum
29 Rent
30 Playthings

DOWN

1 Punt
2 Temeraire
3 Ochre
4 Larwood
5 Neglect
7 Arrow
8 Forbearing
9 Asphodel
14 Astronomer
16 Emulates
18 Lohengrin
20 Needful
21 Devilry
23 Arson
25 Rajah
26 Imps

1933

ACROSS

1 Cutting
5 Demerit
9 Medoc
10 Memento
11 Loo
12 Clove
13 Nonpareil
16 Mon
17 Lisle
18 Extremity
20 Pointless
24 Basis
27 Two
28 Grandsire
32 Whale
33 Air
34 Kindred
35 Owing
36 Numbers
37 Rampant

DOWN

1 Comical
2 Tedious
3 Inclement
4 Garonne
5 Demon
6 Mamba
7 Ranee
8 Trolley
14 Par
15 Ram
19 Elbow room
20 Pigskin
21 Nun
22 LMS
23 Steamer
25 Stamina
26 Sleight
29 Annam
30 Dirge
31 Indus

1934

ACROSS

1 Royal Academy
8 Emperor
9 Parsnip
11 Russian
12 Slimmer
13 Guest
14 Tradesman
16 Recipient
19 Ghoul
21 Tantara
23 Rolling
24 Reigate
25 Ananias
26 Amphitheatre

DOWN

1 Riposte
2 Yorkist
3 Lorgnette
4 Capes
5 Dormice
6 Minimum
7 Refrigerator
10 Phrenologist
15 Alternate
17 Confirm
18 Pharaoh
19 Gallant
20 Orifice
22 Avert

1935

ACROSS

1 Quarterstaff
8 Headman
9 Waldorf
12 Rain
13 Huron
14 Lily
17 Cognate
18 Kinsman
19 Mollusc
22 Shellac
24 Opal
25 Acorn
26 Kohl
29 Shallop
31 Conform
32 Merrythought

DOWN

1 Quaking
2 Army
3 Tonsure
4 Rowlock
5 Toll
6 Fir
7 Short commons
10 Opium
11 Flying column
15 Caius
20 Liana
21 Cockpit
22 Sirocco
23 Lookout
27 Slur
28 Snag
30 Him

1936

ACROSS

7 Polynesia
8 Brief
10 Diplomat
11 Punish
12 Eden
13 Falsetto
16 Daft
18 Godless
20 Overall
22 Puma
24 Fullness
26 Last
29 Oblige
30 Larboard
31 Onion
32 Assurance

DOWN

1 Bogie
2 Eyelid
3 Beamends
4 Distaff
5 Grandeur
6 Versatile
9 Opal
14 Atom
15 Columbine
17 Asps
19 Lollipop
21 Valorous
23 Useless
25 Ewes
27 Slogan
28 Brace

1937

ACROSS

1 Albania
5 Catspaw
9 Tonight
10 Gurnard
11 Rosette
15 Ejector
19 Haste
21 Pumice
22 Zenith
23 Awake
24 Minuet
25 Barrie
26 Raise
29 Uttered
32 Clapper
36 Umbrage
37 Tigress
38 Proverb
39 Heronry

DOWN

1 Actor
2 Bones
3 Night
4 Anthea
5 Cygnet
6 Three
7 Plait
8 Wader
12 Oculist
13 Epicure
14 Theatre
16 Jezebel
17 Cantrip
18 Outside
20 Spahi
27 Adverb
28 Scotch
29 Usurp
30 Taboo
31 Reade
33 Anger
34 Preen
35 Rusty

1938

ACROSS

1 Pawnbroker
9 Base
10 Goods train
11 Gather
12 Salve
15 Hasty
18 Panic
19 Expunge
20 Mania
21 Diana
22 Swansea
23 Night
24 Lodge
26 Seine
29 Ermine
31 Touch and go
32 Grit
33 Overridden

DOWN

2 Avon
3 Nudist
4 Rates
5 Kraal
6 Range
7 Cash in hand
8 Depreciate
13 Appease
14 Venison
15 Ham and eggs
16 Senegambia
17 Yeast
18 Pedal
25 Opined
26 Set to
27 Inure
28 Ether
30 Ogre

1939

ACROSS

5 Hubbub
8 Solitude
9 Walrus
10 Last year
11 Tale
14 Despatch rider
19 Irish
22 Delight
23 Trace
25 Musical chairs
31 Wren
33 Half time
34 On fire
35 Mourning
36 Beagle

DOWN

1 Solace
2 Tiptop
3 Purest
4 Dearth
5 Hawaii
6 Bolster
7 Usual
12 Aria
13 Echo
15 Andes
16 Colic
17 Regal
18 Ditch
20 Stow
21 Game
24 Cunning
26 Impede
27 At home
28 Colour
29 Acting
30 Romany
32 Ranee

1940

ACROSS

1 Regulated
6 Cabot
9 Shipowner
10 Melon
11 Gap
12 Segregate
15 Agate
16 Jewel
19 Hobbs
21 Ups
22 But
23 Caste
24 Surge
26 Assam
27 Commander
31 Owl
32 Twain
33 Allotment
35 Ruddy
36 Hopscotch

DOWN

1 Rests
2 Going
3 Loose
4 Ten
5 Dirge
6 Compasses
7 Beleaguer
8 Tennessee
13 Rye
14 Athos
16 Jobmaster
17 Withstand
18 Luckmoney
20 Bream
25 Urn
27 Clash
28 Antic
29 Dwelt
30 Ratch
34 Lop

1941

ACROSS

1 Light rays
6 Cubic
9 Guardsman
10 Blade
11 Contour
12 Arraign
13 Aft
14 Parasol
17 Hothead
19 Chimera
22 Harelip
24 Nay
25 Opacity
26 Deflate
29 Idiot
30 Alabaster
31 Lance
32 Satanical

DOWN

1 Logic
2 Grain
3 Tedious
4 Admiral
5 Sun-bath
6 Cabaret
7 Beau-ideal
8 Cleaned up
14 Pictorial
15 Ruination
16 Our
18 Ova
20 Epistle
21 Any rags
22 Hydrant
23 Refrain
27 Antic
28 Enrol

1942

ACROSS

1 Redruth
5 Crowbar
9 Blossom
10 Palermo
11 Sweeten
15 Largess
19 Medal
21 Toffee
22 Myriad
23 Ratio
24 Flicks
25 Needle
26 Ophir
29 Anodyne
32 Mystery
36 The bush
37 Aquatic
38 Heathen
39 Titania

DOWN

1 Rebus
2 Drone
3 Upset
4 Humane
5 Cupola
6 Oiler
7 Barge
8 Roots
12 Woollen
13 Effaced
14 Emerson
16 Almonry
17 Garment
18 Smaller
20 Ditch
27 Peahen
28 Impact
29 Aitch
30 Opera
31 Youth
33 Squat
34 Eaten
35 Yucca

1943

ACROSS

1 Tobacco
5 Postbag
9 Realist
10 Cartoon
11 Wallpaper
12 Genii
13 Niece
15 Knowledge
17 Disdained
19 Ratal
22 Banjo
23 Wandering
25 Overawe
26 Neglect
27 Scenery
28 Wheedle

DOWN

1 Throw-in
2 Braille
3 Crisp
4 Outspoken
5 Pacer
6 Straggler
7 Browned
8 Genuine
14 Evaporate
16 Old and new
17 Dubious
18 Sincere
20 Tail-end
21 Legatee
23 Weedy
24 Eagle

1944

ACROSS

1 Long Island
8 Idle
10 Democratic
11 Ruin
12 Edge
15 New York
18 Alice
19 Erect
20 Breve
21 Ingot
22 Poser
23 Union
24 Green
25 Usher
26 Earnest
30 Pelt
33 Pros
34 Watertight
35 Kiwi
36 Garden gate

DOWN

2 Omen
3 Glove
4 Surly
5 Actor
6 Dice
7 Flag
9 Breaking up
10 Diving bell
13 Dress-shirt
14 Enterprise
15 **Neptune**
16 Ocean
17 Keep out
20 Briar
27 Aster
28 Norse
29 Sling
31 Evil
32 Twig
33 Phut

1945   1946   1947

ACROSS

1 Broadcloth
9 Rose
10 Sanatorium
11 Dented
12 Channel
15 Burglar
16 Realm
17 Nile
18 Lino
19 Pause
21 Paschal
22 Hard nut
24 Reader
27 On the spree
28 Coal
29 Expedition

DOWN

2 Ream
3 Amazon
4 Crooner
5 Omit
6 Humdrum
7 Postillion
8 Tenderfoot
12 Conspiracy
13 Able seaman
14 Legal
15 Blush
19 Padrone
20 East End
23 Despot
25 Stop
26 Zero

ACROSS

1 Ought
4 Shoeblack
9 Science
10 Low diet
11 Ella
12 Frail
13 Itch
16 Brevity
17 Eyebrow
19 Relying
22 Colonel
24 Park
25 Tours
26 Skye
29 Ortolan
30 Clouded
31 Groundsel
32 Rayon

DOWN

1 Oyster bar
2 Ghillie
3 Tiny
4 Swear by
5 Oil pipe
6 Bows
7 Aviator
8 Ketch
14 Visit
15 Keble
18 Willesden
20 Loretto
21 Grounds
22 Caracal
23 Nakedly
24 Prong
27 Design
28 Tour

ACROSS

1 Hobart
4 Scimitar
9 Lordly
10 Duelling
12 Dais
13 Waste
14 Meal
17 Wrack and ruin
20 Recollection
23 Pard
24 Attic
25 Rose
28 Undertow
29 Marrow
30 Eternity
31 Clammy

DOWN

1 Hull down
2 Barbican
3 Rely
5 Counter claim
6 Male
7 Toiler
8 Regale
11 Rainbow trout
15 Skies
16 Piece
18 Kilogram
19 Under way
21 Spruce
22 Bridle
26 Arun
27 Fall

1948　　1949　　1950

1948

ACROSS

1 Mole cast
5 Stop it
9 Milky way
10 Repast
11 Smelting
12 Writhe
14 White woman
18 Dark cranny
22 Linnet
23 Twice two
24 Twaite
25 Platform
26 Reseda
27 Asphodel

DOWN

1 Mimosa
2 Lilies
3 Coyote
4 Staunch pal
6 The crown
7 Playtime
8 To the end
13 Stone walls
15 Idolater
16 Iron bars
17 Accepted
19 Scotch
20 Stroud
21 Pommel

1949

ACROSS

1 Clydeside
8 Automatically
11 Abbé
12 Toddy
13 Pier
16 Thereon
17 Eastern
18 Oculist
20 Sea wall
21 Ruby
22 Rival
23 Jinn
26 Dead reckoning
27 Hands down

DOWN

2 Loot
3 Dragoon
4 Spindle
5 Dram
6 Hubble-bubbles
7 Alliterations
9 Dart-board
10 Brandling
14 Debit
15 Assam
19 Tail end
20 Stacked
24 Idea
25 Snow

1950

ACROSS

1 Forth
4 Abandoned
9 Druidic
11 Venison
12 Ruin
13 Quart
14 Tiny
17 Tongue-twister
19 Unforgettable
21 Clan
22 Cheep
23 Jinn
26 Brazier
27 Thistle
28 Twentieth
29 Falls

DOWN

1 Federated
2 Reunion
3 Hide
5 Advertisement
6 Done
7 Nastier
8 Dandy
10 Counter-charge
15 Buffs
16 State
18 Queen bees
19 Unaware
20 Bristol
21 Cabot
24 List
25 Riff

1951

ACROSS

1 Obstinately
9 Leer
10 Aggravating
11 Horn
14 Algebra
17 Lever
18 Proof
19 Cause
20 Tyrol
21 Loser
22 Exact
23 Lyons
24 Knife
25 Sceptre
29 Yoke
32 Interviewer
33 Ring
34 Undertaking

DOWN

2 Bags
3 Tyre
4 Novel
5 Tithe
6 Liner
7 Hero-worship
8 Transformer
12 Platelayers
13 Overlooking
14 Artless
15 Blunt
16 Apelike
19 Crave
26 Canon
27 Piece
28 Rivet
30 Deck
31 Keen

1952

ACROSS

1 Willesden
9 Wesley
10 Kingston
11 Common
12 Scribe
14 Boot
15 Aural
16 Banana
18 Gilbert
21 Mashona
24 Nine up
26 Elgar
30 Room
31 Awaken
32 Ossian
33 Sullivan
34 Humour
35 Meandered

DOWN

2 Idiocy
3 Loggia
4 Setter
5 Ennoble
6 Pelota
7 Plumbago
8 Dying away
11 Cobra
13 Bude
17 Agincourt
19 Lonesome
20 Ripon
22 Shaw
23 Demesne
25 Uranus
27 Gallon
28 Rapine
29 Sedate

1953

ACROSS

1 Concertina
6 Sloe
10 Facer
11 Microtome
12 Eschalot
13 Theft
15 Twister
17 Epigram
19 Thyroid
21 The pale
22 Organ
24 Clematis
27 Apprehend
28 Lease
29 Yo-yo
30 Assessment

DOWN

1 Cafe
2 Necessity
3 Earth
4 Tumbler
5 Necktie
7 Loose
8 Even temper
9 Lost time
14 Stationary
16 Trounced
18 Reanimate
20 Duchess
21 Treadle
23 Gipsy
25 Atlas
26 Jest

1954

ACROSS

1 Artificial
9 Spar
10 Capability
11 Delete
12 Capstan
15 Lynched
16 Lagos
17 Nail
18 Mesh
19 Cried
21 Treacle
22 Dress up
24 Boiler
27 Kind hearts
28 Eric
29 Angry crowd

DOWN

2 Roar
3 Images
4 Initial
5 Iris
6 Lay-days
7 Speechless
8 Friendship
12 Constables
13 Price limit
14 Nacre
15 Lowed
19 Clarkia
20 Droshky
23 Sea air
25 Snug
26 Stow

1955

ACROSS

1 Fishing-rod
9 Tour
10 Post-mortem
11 Oregon
12 Essen
15 Clerk
18 Speed
19 Routine
20 Nubia
21 Drive
22 Alberta
23 Extol
24 Nidus
26 Germs
29 Weevil
31 Auctioneer
32 Reel
33 Despondent

DOWN

2 Idol
3 Hot air
4 Noose
5 Rates
6 Demon
7 Tongue-tied
8 Grenadiers
13 Stubble
14 Epigram
15 Canker-worm
16 Embittered
17 Kraal
18 Sedan
25 Ironed
26 Gland
27 Rocks
28 Sligo
30 Keen

1956

ACROSS

1 Box numbers
9 Bale
10 Advertiser
11 Glut
12 Rally
15 Valet
18 Vowel
19 Incense
20 Canoe
21 Reeds
22 Rousing
23 Nones
24 Error
25 Stags
28 Pore
31 Long Island
32 Oast
33 Delegation

DOWN

2 Odds
3 Noel
4 Meter
5 Easel
6 Surly
7 Fallow deer
8 Fertiliser
13 Account
14 Lending
15 Vacant plot
16 Linen-press
17 Tiers
18 Verge
25 Salad
26 Annul
27 Sting
29 Flat
30 Undo

1957   1958   1959

ACROSS

1 Chopper
5 Tobacco
9 Bed and breakfast
10 Eggs
11 Holly
12 Harp
15 Sappers
16 Sleuths
17 Banking
19 Retired
21 Acid
22 Misty
23 Isis
26 Singing practice
27 Earthen
28 Pressed

DOWN

1 Cobwebs
2 Old age pensioner
3 Pink
4 Ribbons
5 Trellis
6 Bike
7 Characteristics
8 Octopus
13 Devil
14 Jetty
17 Brassie
18 Going on
19 Rat-trap
20 Descend
24 Fish
25 Acre

ACROSS

1 Pawnbroker
9 Thou
10 Down and out
11 Ordeal
12 Hiker
15 Satyr
18 Music
19 Echidna
20 Gable
21 Doubt
22 Liberia
23 Aphis
24 Mayor
26 Stoep
29 Limpet
31 Rectangles
32 Noes
33 Paratroops

DOWN

2 Atom
3 Ninety
4 Ranch
5 Knock
6 Rotor
7 Shrewsbury
8 Duplicator
13 Inhabit
14 Endorse
15 Signalling
16 Tub-thumper
17 Reels
18 Madam
25 Adagio
26 Strap
27 Oscar
28 Plant
30 Peep

ACROSS

1 At first blush
9 Unheard
10 Tonnage
11 Thaw
12 Verne
13 Judo
16 Retract
17 Scutage
18 Incubus
21 Goliath
23 Gong
24 Dally
25 Calm
28 Reunion
29 Ominous
30 Breeches-buoy

DOWN

1 Athwart
2 Foam
3 Red heat
4 Tetanus
5 Lone
6 Scapula
7 Butter-fingers
8 Before the mast
14 Mamba
15 Bully
19 Conquer
20 Staunch
21 Gallows
22 Analogy
26 Hide
27 Lieu

1960

ACROSS

1 Mother Hubbard
10 Octopus
11 Conform
12 Neat
13 Proud
14 Star
17 Needles
18 Homeric
19 Samovar
22 Swindon
24 Rose
25 Usher
26 Well
29 Example
30 Transit
31 Secretary bird

DOWN

2 Outrage
3 Hope
4 Resorts
5 Uncouth
6 Bank
7 Rooster
8 Downing Street
9 American cloth
15 Slave
16 Ambit
20 Mistake
21 Respect
22 Swelter
23 Dresser
27 Spar
28 Lamb

1961

ACROSS

1 Colossal
5 Barbed
9 Bachelor
10 Blacks
12 Electrode
13 Waste
14 Pass
16 Donated
19 Mandate
21 Fret
24 Rathe
25 Stripling
27 Viewer
28 Quartern
29 Resets
30 Dementia

DOWN

1 Cobweb
2 Locker
3 Spent
4 Amorous
6 Allowance
7 Backsets
8 Descends
11 Weed
15 Amazement
17 Improver
18 Knotless
20 Ease
21 Fortune
22 Digest
23 Agenda
26 Purge

1962

ACROSS

7 Rob the
   mail-coach
8 Western
10 Culprit
11 Donor
12 Folly
14 Snubs
15 Yoke
16 Dray
17 Pelt
19 Beam
21 Steel
22 Dingy
23 Judas
25 Cruiser
26 Tensile
27 Reformed convict

DOWN

1 Power of attorney
2 Stately
3 Beard
4 Flour
5 Company
6 Scribbling-block
9 Nose
10 Cord
13 Yokel
14 Salad
17 Peridot
18 Tour
19 Boat
20 Missive
23 Jemmy
24 Senor

1963

ACROSS

1 Mother-of-pearl
10 Iceberg
11 Georgia
12 Hero
13 Token
14 Sign
17 Hand-out
18 Trident
19 Useless
22 Elastic
24 Even
25 Sneak
26 Sari
29 Avocado
30 Trefoil
31 Penny-farthing

DOWN

2 Overrun
3 Hoes
4 Ragwort
5 Pigment
6 Eros
7 Ragtime
8 Lighthouseman
9 Magnetic field
15 Poker
16 Midas
20 Eyesore
21 Send-off
22 Exactor
23 Tea-gown
27 Barn
28 Mesh

1964

ACROSS

1 Hard and fast rule
9 Misfits
10 Arsenic
11 Elba
12 Flier
13 Emil
16 Sternly
17 Residue
18 Wickets
21 Blanket
23 Year
24 Fanny
25 Inch
28 Tallied
29 Billion
30 The thread of life

DOWN

1 Hammers away
   at it
2 Risible
3 Avid
4 Display
5 Amateur
6 Tosh
7 Unnamed
8 Excellent chance
14 Ended
15 Essay
19 Charlie
20 Swaddle
21 Bone-bed
22 Kon-tiki
26 Wish
27 Clef

1965

ACROSS

1 Sable
4 Duplicate
8 Actaeon
9 Iron age
10 Ewer
11 Perch
12 Left
15 Yorkshire grit
17 Begging letter
20 Love
21 Nappy
22 Avid
25 Grocers
26 Armenia
27 Title-page
28 Theme

DOWN

1 Slate club
2 Battery
3 Even
4 Danger signals
5 Icon
6 Amateur
7 Exert
9 Inclined plane
13 Frail
14 Jetty
16 Third-rate
18 Give out
19 Revenge
20 Light
23 Nene
24 Emit

1966   1967   1968

ACROSS

1 Perpignan
9 Cavour
10 Decimated
11 Felloe
12 Leviathan
13 All set
17 Yet
19 Acushla
20 Run down
21 May
23 Resume
27 Decalogue
28 Thirst
29 Stalemate
30 Lutine
31 Crackling

DOWN

2 Eleven
3 Philip
4 Granta
5 Acetate
6 Tamerlane
7 Collision
8 Argentina
14 Fairy-tale
15 Outskirts
16 Thomasina
17 Yam
18 Try
22 Abetter
24 Gallic
25 Formal
26 Justin

ACROSS

8 Bait
9 Aga
10 Enamel
11 Orange
12 Initiate
13 On the usual lines
15 Wealthy
17 Adoring
20 A law unto
himself
23 Wrangler
25 Nudist
26 Return
27 Ely
28 Neon

DOWN

1 Barren
2 Stendhal
3 Careful handling
4 Carious
5 Devilled kidneys
6 Tahiti
7 Felt
14 Eon
16 Ell
18 Resident
19 Courier
21 Wensum
22 Lesson
24 Rhea

ACROSS

1 Slave labour
8 Lack of sleep
11 Arid
12 Dodo
13 Peerage
15 Attires
16 Swiss
17 Inns
18 No go
19 Armed
21 Hot dogs
22 Derides
23 Este
26 Peso
27 Evening star
28 Gretna Green

DOWN

2 Load
3 Vikings
4 Left
5 Billets
6 Used
7 Lamplighter
8 Live in state
9 Poor soldier
10 Non-stop show
14 Ewers
15 Asked
19 Against
20 Dear sir
24 Ever
25 Inca
26 Pace

1969

ACROSS

1 Double flat
6 Cain
9 Clover-leaf
10 View
13 Serious
15 Ostler
16 Mother
17 Lacking interest
18 Desire
20 Ensign
21 Scrooge
22 Vein
25 Artificial
26 Rule
27 Debentures

DOWN

1 Dace
2 Upon
3 Lieder
4 Falling into line
5 Alarum
7 Arithmetic
8 New writing
11 Bowled over
12 Stock-still
13 Seniors
14 Someone
19 Ecarte
20 Egoist
23 Pier
24 Plus

1970

ACROSS

1 British Rail
8 In great part
11 Owns
12 Yawn
13 Tribune
15 Supreme
16 Sweat
17 Need
18 Waif
19 & 21
   Train drivers
22 Beechen
23 Ache
26 Once
27 Treasonable
28 In a small way

DOWN

2 Runs
3 Tartans
4 Shaw
5 Rips out
6 Ivry
7 Rottingdean
8 Inside right
9 Tape-machine
10 Index finger
14 Ewers
15 Sahib
19 Trojans
20 Netball
24 Erin
25 Rosa
26 Olla

1971

ACROSS

6 Television fan
8 Appear
9 Eyesight
10 Ton
11 Merino
12 Congeals
14 Mangled
16 Actress
20 Pitcairn
23 Menial
24 Ida
25 Sneaking
26 Newark
27 Right at the end

DOWN

1 Altering
2 Overtone
3 Essence
4 Modern
5 Office
6 Tipped a winner
7 No holds barred
13 Got
15 Lea
17 Comanche
18 Renowned
19 Knights
21 Change
22 Idiots

1972

ACROSS

1 Comatose
5 Spited
9 Separate
10 Glared
11 Round off
12 Asleep
14 Second home
18 Contention
22 U-boats
23 Maudling
24 Armlet
25 Division
26 Enlist
27 Snuggery

DOWN

1 Castro
2 Map out
3 Tirade
4 Set of teeth
6 Palisade
7 Turned on
8 Didapper
13 Coloration
15 Accurate
16 Informal
17 Heathens
19 Idling
20 Finite
21 Agency

1973

ACROSS

1 Hard core
5 Proper
9 Soft soap
10 Fibres
11 Elegists
13 Enigma
14 Shy
16 Entrée
19 Rioting
20 League
21 Gem
26 Poncho
27 Rest-home
28 Hat-box
29 Vibrates
30 Desert
31 Cat's-eyes

DOWN

1 Hashed
2 Rifled
3 Cassia
4 Reacts
6 Reigning
7 Périgord
8 Reshaped
12 Shatter
15 Pie
16 End
17 Slipshod
18 Magnates
19 Rush hour
22 Medina
23 Storms
24 Costly
25 Census

1974

ACROSS

1 Plum-duff
5 Stamen
9 Last look
10 Trends
11 Calliope
12 Gaming
14 Vigorously
18 Mosquitoes
22 Tarzan
23 Salic Law
24 Thebes
25 Sibilant
26 Rotate
27 Anisette

DOWN

1 Policy
2 Unsold
3 Dulcie
4 Footprints
6 Tarragon
7 Mantissa
8 Nosegays
13 Moderation
15 Imitator
16 Esurient
17 Subagent
19 Lilies
20 Pliant
21 Swathe

1975

ACROSS
1 Allowed
5 Sampler
9 Lounges
10 Reynard
11 Endorsing
12 Ladle
13 Layer
15 Live wires
17 Ancestral
19 Rufus
22 Dwell
23 Mint sauce
25 Oxonian
26 Infidel
27 Draught
28 Ensured

DOWN
1 & 17 All well and good
2 Laundry
3 Wager
4 Distiller
5 Sprig
6 Mayflower
7 Leander
8 Redress
14 Resolving
16 Valentine
17 *See 1 down*
18 Cremona
20 Founder
21 Spelled
23 Manet
24 Sifts

1976

ACROSS
1 Steam-whistle
8 Log-book
9 Beef tea
11 Plateau
12 Telstar
13 Posit
14 Music-hall
16 In the know
19 Gulch
21 Genoese
23 Handsaw
24 Reactor
25 Atelier
26 Secret treaty

DOWN
1 Signals
2 Erodent
3 Make-up man
4 Habit
5 Shellac
6 Letitia
7 Klipspringer
10 April showers
15 Saw the air
17 Tonnage
18 Elector
19 Gunnera
20 Lustily
22 Egret

1977

ACROSS
1 & 5 Common or garden
9 Auditors
10 Hansom
12 Green-room
13 Elgin
14 Bask
16 Thereat
19 & 21 Fatigue duty
24 Ounce
25 Shake-down
27 Repeal
28 Revoking
29 Esther
30 Etcetera

DOWN
1 & 17 Change of course
2 Madder
3 Often
4 Oarlock
6 Abasement
7 Designed
8 Nominate
11 Emit
15 Aggregate
17 *See 1 down*
18 Stand pat
20 East
21 Dearest
22 Notice
23 Enigma
26 Elope

1978

ACROSS

1 In the wings
6 Plum
10 Copra
11 Very light
12 Rent-free
13 Earth
15 Implore
17 Sultana
19 Elector
21 Habitué
22 Ladle
24 Gorgeous
27 Gas mantle
28 Elder
29 Pays
30 Call it a day

DOWN

1 Inch
2 Top people
3 Exact
4 Inverse
5 Girders
7 Lager
8 Matchmaker
9 Glee club
14 Give a leg up
16 On the mat
18 Astounded
20 Regatta
21 Harwell
23 Dusty
25 Evert
26 Fray

1979

ACROSS

1 Dispatch
5 Swathe
9 Boasting
10 Coarse
11 Indicate
12 Aghast
14 Manicurist
18 Adroitness
22 Dotage
23 Increase
24 Abadan
25 Undercut
26 Laymen
27 Leftists

DOWN

1 Dobbin
2 Shandy
3 Attack
4 Constrains
6 & 19 Wrongful
     arrest
7 Terrapin
8 Edentate
13 Dissonance
15 Handrail
16 Brittany
17 Disgrace
19 *See 6*
20 Marcus
21 Deaths

1980

ACROSS

1 Landslide
8 Opening gambit
11 Arch
12 Pixie
13 Rhea
16 Peacock
17 Explain
18 Hitchin
20 Blondes
21 Dual
22 Aitch
23 Urdu
26 In sight of land
27 Loadstone

DOWN

2 Arno
3 Dunkirk
4 Lignite
5 Dame
6 Special trains
7 Right and wrong
9 Lampshade
10 Magnesium
14 Mocha
15 Spoon
19 Neighed
20 Back out
24 Lido
25 Flan

1981

ACROSS

1 Guillemot
9 Cocoon
10 Admiralty
11 Keynes
12 Celestial
13 Uglier
17 Peg
19 Arundel
20 Airship
21 Yap
23 Making
27 Saxifrage
28 Permit
29 Volleying
30 Lascar
31 Petrol can

DOWN

2 Undies
3 Loiter
4 Ecarte
5 Oatcake
6 Cover girl
7 Downright
8 One stripe
14 Warm spell
15 Quakerish
16 Identical
17 Ply
18 Gap
22 Abalone
24 Miller
25 Argyll
26 Agenda

1982

ACROSS

1 Money to spare
8 Erratic
9 Accrues
11 Suspect
12 Opaline
13 Ropes
14 Architect
16 Houseless
19 Delhi
21 Useless
23 Miscall
24 Stretto
25 Theresa
26 Changed sides

DOWN

1 Marks up
2 Nutmegs
3 Yacht race
4 Otago
5 Peccavi
6 Routine
7 Leisure hours
10 Sweet William
15 Casemates
17 Unearth
18 Everton
19 Distend
20 Loafers
22 Shone

1983

ACROSS

1 Upper crust
9 Dior
10 Motherwell
11 Listen
12 Parsons
15 Ageless
16 Eagle
17 Digs
18 Gaga
19 Acres
21 Set fire
22 Strayed
24 Rubble
27 Not one of us
28 Ague
29 Amendments

DOWN

2 Poop
3 Ethics
4 Carline
5 Used
6 Tillage
7 Little Mary
8 Grandstand
12 Pedestrian
13 Right about
14 Sauce
15 Aloes
19 Armenia
20 Stunned
23 Alcove
25 Stye
26 Bust

1984   1985   1986

ACROSS

1 Gillingham
6 Oslo
10 & 11 On the tight side
12 Fritters
13 Charm
15 Rustles
17 Artisan
19 Caravan
21 Pinnace
22 Ormer
24 Trap-door
27 Signifies
28 Break
29 Etty
30 Credit card

DOWN

1 & 14 Good gracious me
2 Late riser
3 Inert
4 Gutters
5 Augusta
7 Spica
8 Overmantel
9 Stockton
14 *See 1 down*
16 Live rail
18 Soap opera
20 Nattier
21 Praised
23 Might
25 Debut
26 Skid

ACROSS

1 Tipster
5 Refuses
9 Parents
10 Prowler
11 Olive
12 Last stand
13 Assails
14 Sitters
16 Dusters
19 Created
22 Classroom
24 Terse
25 Dribble
26 Reeling
27 Daggers
28 Settees

DOWN

1 Tapioca
2 Parries
3 Tangerine
4 Results
5 Repasts
6 Flows
7 Salvage
8 Strides
15 Treatment
16 Decoded
17 Staying
18 Showers
19 Cameras
20 Termite
21 Dredges
23 Sabre

ACROSS

1 Seasoned
5 Scorns
9 Air-strip
10 Snatch
11 Explicit
12 Kimono
14 Magistrate
18 Conscience
22 Bracts
23 Legatine
24 Acetic
25 Stalking
26 Design
27 Pretence

DOWN

1 Slater
2 Abrupt
3 Outdid
4 Eliminated
6 Convicts
7 Rational
8 Schooner
13 Winchester
15 Scabbard
16 Invaders
17 Scathing
19 Ballet
20 Lilian
21 League

1987

ACROSS

1 Made a mess
9 Mirage
10 Come clean
11 Assail
12 Plastered
13 Armada
17 Nip
19 In the first place
20 Lei
21 Honest
25 Star-gazer
26 Serial
27 Contender
28 Outfit
29 Ostracise

DOWN

2 Atolls
3 Ever so
4 Miller
5 Stage directions
6 Pin-stripe
7 Catamaran
8 Tell tales
14 Tight spot
15 At any rate
16 Messianic
17 Nil
18 Psi
22 Writer
23 Tannic
24 Recess

1988

ACROSS

1 Lukewarm
5 Spasms
9 Dastardy
10 Atonic
11 Eventide
12 Bearer
14 Fire-blight
18 Overcharge
22 Detour
23 Natation
24 Adonis
25 Sixpence
26 Dotage
27 Integral

DOWN

1 Ledger
2 Kismet
3 Wraith
4 Red-admiral
6 Pot-belly
7 Sentry-go
8 Security
13 Belgravian
15 Bondmaid
16 Beetroot
17 Scouting
19 Magpie
20 Winner
21 Unwell

1989

ACROSS

1 Crowned head
10 Inner
11 Carbonado
12 Discharge
13 Tulsa
14 Abrupt
16 Bogeyman
18 Caviller
20 Bottom
23 Utter
24 Light-year
26 Ranunculi
27 Usual
28 Prayer-wheel

DOWN

2 Rings
3 Warship
4 Encore
5 Horse-box
6 Apostle
7 Bird sanctuary
8 Table-mat
9 Roman numerals
15 Riveting
17 Jealousy
19 Loriner
21 Outrush
22 Uglier
25 Elude

1990

ACROSS

1 Bush fire
5 Wrench
9 All found
10 Age-old
12 Stock size
13 Ratio
14 Flog
16 Trimmed
19 Hammock
21 Bags
24 Colts
25 Holy smoke
27 Nectar
28 Live down
29 Europe
30 In detail

DOWN

1 Braise
2 Sallow
3 Frock
4 Running
6 Regarding
7 Noontime
8 Had words
11 Beat
15 Look sharp
17 Chaconne
18 Small car
20 Kohl
21 Billion
22 Bogota
23 Fennel
26 Siege

1991

ACROSS

1 Stouter
5 Resides
9 Pretend
10 Snapped
11 Insistent
12 Easel
13 Grebe
15 Towcester
17 Discourse
19 Tobit
22 Rumba
23 Abstainer
25 Calling
26 Outrage
27 Strange
28 Earnest

DOWN

1 Sapping
2 Oversee
3 Tiers
4 Red-letter
5 Reset
6 Statement
7 Deposit
8 Saddler
14 Evocation
16 Whetstone
17 Directs
18 Similar
20 Bandage
21 Torment
23 Angle
24 Astir

1992

ACROSS

1 Compose oneself
9 Take off
10 Clutter
11 Auto
12 Break ranks
14 Emerge
15 Agonised
17 Atomiser
18 Assail
21 Antithesis
22 Brag
24 Officer
25 Turn out
26 St Clement Danes

DOWN

1 Cut-rate
2 Make the most
of it
3 Oboe
4 Effort
5 No charge
6 Squareness
7 Let one's hair
down
8 Prised
13 Egoistical
16 Cerebrum
17 Amazon
19 Legates
20 Listen
23 Prod

1993

ACROSS

1 Bombarded
9 Outpost
10 Begrime
11 Ice fall
12 Hands down
14 Hookworm
15 Crimea
17 Clapper
20 Aspire
23 Bonhomie
25 Statutory
26 Onerous
27 Calends
28 Steeple
29 Seediness

DOWN

2 Open air
3 Boredom
4 Remedial
5 Domino
6 Streakers
7 Rotator
8 Stalemate
13 Whippet
15 Clubhouse
16 Ectomorph
18 Eastward
19 Integer
21 Pattern
22 Reredos
24 Issues

1994

ACROSS

7 Bone china
8 Motor
10 Muleteer
11 One way
12 Lead
13 Virginal
15 Unkempt
17 Isolate
20 Sweet pea
22 Inca
25 Arctic
26 Ardennes
27 Onion
28 Sheerness

DOWN

1 Bonus
2 Severe
3 Sheepdip
4 On drive
5 Molehill
6 Bonaparte
9 Hour
14 Answering
16 Ejection
18 Swindles
19 Panache
21 Pack
23 Canine
24 Cease

1995

ACROSS

1 Apple charlotte
9 Maestri
10 Retaken
11 Rosy
12 Thoughtful
14 Drop in
15 Dead-heat
17 Defector
18 Concur
21 String vest
22 Slut
24 Dungeon
25 Leakage
26 Heated argument

DOWN

1 Admired
2 Press conference
3 Etty
4 Height
5 Rerouted
6 Octahedron
7 Take french leave
8 Anklet
13 Disconcert
16 Convened
17 Dosi-do
19 Retreat
20 Ostler
23 Tabu

1996

ACROSS

1 Inheritor
6 Lucre
9 Faction
10 Uniformly
11 Ontario
12 Emanate
13 Straws in the wind
18 Chapter
20 Tabasco
22 Moderator
23 Pfennig
24 Tansy
25 Tender age

DOWN

1 Infamous
2 Huckster
3 Raider
4 Tenuto
5 Regiment
6 Lemonade
7 Crimea
8 Enzyme
14 Waterway
15 Irritant
16 Insignia
17 Duologue
18 Combat
19 Andean
20 Tarpon
21 Breeze

1997

ACROSS

1 Stationed
9 Column
10 Bedridden
11 Gamble
12 Lionesses
13 Plater
17 Eta
19 Brother
20 Contest
21 Eat
23 Umpire
27 Registers
28 Thatch
29 Backcloth
30 Ranker
31 Represent

DOWN

2 Thesis
3 Tiring
4 Oldest
5 Element
6 Totalling
7 Sunbather
8 Integrate
14 About turn
15 Complaint
16 Character
17 Ere
18 Act
22 Average
24 Licker
25 Stalls
26 Croton

1998

ACROSS

1 Take exception to
9 Waterfowl
10 Posse
11 Rehouse
12 Tel Aviv
13 Rue
14 Falsely
17 Dweller
19 Thimble
22 Morpeth
24 Lea
25 Elm-tree
26 Tamable
28 Get on
29 Ting-a-ling
30 Have two left feet

DOWN

1 Tower of strength
2 Ketch
3 En route
4 Cookery
5 Piloted
6 Impulse
7 Nashville
8 One over the eight
15 Leitmotiv
16 Lil
18 Woo
20 Baronet
21 Electro
22 Matinee
23 Rampart
27 Brine

1999 2000 2001

1999

2000

2001

2002

ACROSS

1 Stepson
5 Recover
9 Augment
10 Non-stop
11 Stonecrop
12 Niche
13 Apsis
15 Offerings
17 Overissue
19 Merit
22 Staff
23 Redresser
25 Routing
26 Acreage
27 Elector
28 Earnest

DOWN

1 Swansea
2 Engross
3 Scene
4 Notorious
5 Ran up
6 Conundrum
7 Vatican
8 Repress
14 Skinflint
16 Fieldfare
17 Observe
18 Erasure
20 Roseate
21 Torment
23 Roger
24 Error

2003

ACROSS

1 Twitch
4 Whole hog
10 Alder
11 Inamorata
12 Synonym
13 Tickers
14 Insurance claim
17 Patchwork quilt
21 Enfield
23 Heigh-ho
24 Accordion
25 Baton
26 Badinage
27 Seaway

DOWN

1 Transfix
2 Indonesia
3 Coroner
5 Heart-searching
6 Lioncel
7 Heave
8 Gdansk
9 Diamond wedding
15 Irish stew
16 Attorney
18 Chevron
19 Quibble
20 Bedaub
22 Faced

2004

ACROSS

1 Long-suffering
9 Recollect
10 In fun
11 Eyrie
12 Gang
13 Thor
15 Transit
17 Theorem
18 Arcadia
20 Succeed
21 Lint
22 Edgy
23 Might
26 Flank
27 Brilliant
28 Tender-hearted

DOWN

1 Larger-than-life
2 Nicer
3 Silverside
4 Freight
5 Extinct
6 Ibid
7 Gift horse
8 Unpremeditated
14 Peach Melba
16 Ascendant
19 Audible
20 Sky-high
24 Graft
25 Skin

2005

ACROSS

1 Knees-up
5 Repaint
9 Regards
10 Lollard
11 *(no clue)*
12 Green
13 Nepal
15 Hedonists
17 *(no clue)*
19 Motif
22 Tulle
23 Pacemaker
25 *(no clue)*
26 Igneous
27 Nonstop
28 Necktie

DOWN

1 Keratin
2 Egg-flip
3 Scrag
4 Pistachio
5 Ralph
6 Polygonum
7 In a mess
8 Tidings
14 Lashes out
16 Deduction
17 Catch on
18 Only son
20 Take out
21 Foresee
23 Pay up
24 Manic

The three solution words omitted from this puzzle (two nine-letter words and one seven-letter word) can be deduced from the letters given through other solution words crossing them, together with the content of this book. Having deduced the solution words, compile your own cryptic clue for one, two or all of the words and send them – together with your name and phone number – to:

Val Gilbert,
Daily Telegraph
80 Years of Cryptic Crosswords
  Competition,
c/o Pan Macmillan,
20 New Wharf Road,
London N1 9RR

by Monday 30 May 2005

The best clues will be included and credited in *The Daily Telegraph*'s special birthday crossword to be printed on Saturday 30 July 2005.

Visit www.crossword.telegraph.co.uk to find out more about the *Telegraph Crossword Society*, the home of word games for the cognoscenti – including an exclusive series of crosswords from *The Telegraph* archives to mark the 80th anniversary.